Country Paths and City Sidewalks

The Art of J. G. Brown

MARTHA J. HOPPIN

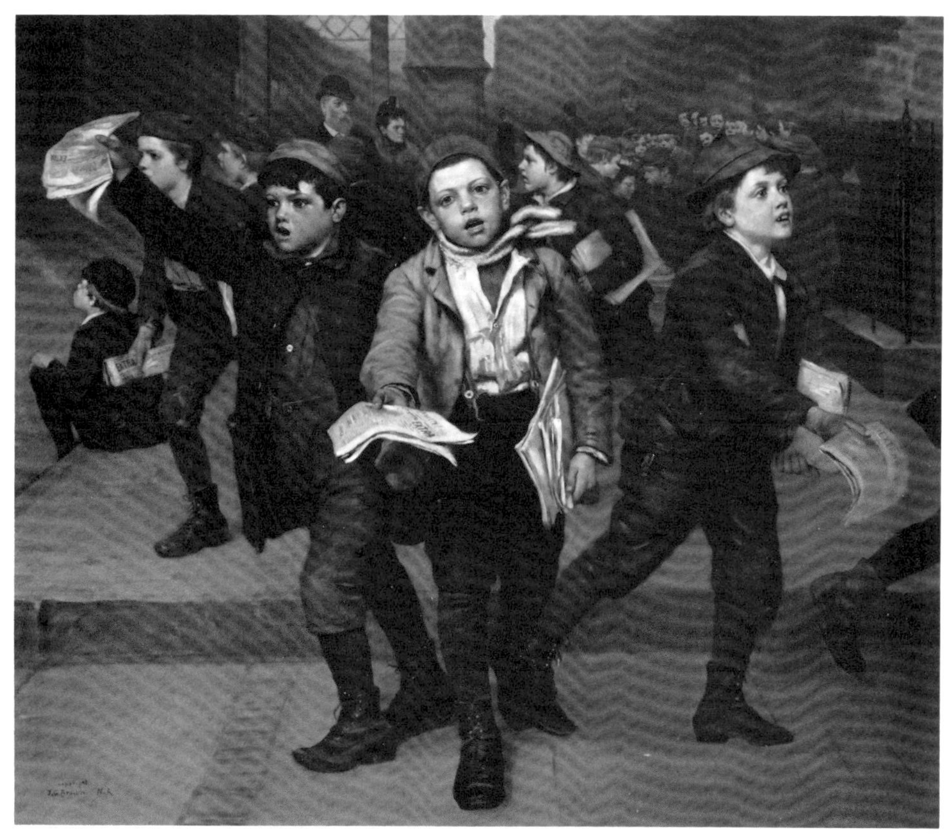

GEORGE WALTER VINCENT SMITH ART MUSEUM

SPRINGFIELD, MASSACHUSETTS

This exhibition is supported by a grant from the National Endowment for the Arts, a federal agency.

The operation of the George Walter Vincent Smith Art Museum and all of its programs is made possible, in part, with support from the Massachusetts Council on the Arts and Humanities, a state agency.

EXHIBITION ITINERARY:

George Walter Vincent Smith Art Museum
Springfield, Massachusetts
March 19-May 21, 1989

National Academy of Design, New York
July 10-September 10, 1989

Joslyn Art Museum, Omaha, Nebraska
October 13-December 3, 1989

PHOTO CREDITS:

Berry-Hill Galleries, Inc.: cover and fig. 51
Christie's: title page and fig. 15
Hirschl and Adler Galleries, Inc.: figs. 39, 55
Kennedy Galleries, Inc.: figs. 42, 23
Spanierman Gallery: figs. 40, 17, 32
Galleries Maurice Sternberg, Chicago: figs. 29, 31
Photographs for works not listed were provided by lenders

Designed by Deborah Hewitt
Edited by Debra Gorlin
Typeset by Debbie's Type, Westfield, Massachusetts
Printed by The John C. Otto Company, East Longmeadow, Massachusetts

ISBN: 0-916746-14-3
Library of Congress card number: 89-060320

Cover: **Young Girl in a New York Garden,** 1871, from the Private Collection of Mr. and Mrs. Charles O. Smith, Jr.

Title page: **Extra,** c. 1889, Dr. and Mrs. Kenneth Blau

FOREWORD

The George Walter Vincent Smith Art Museum is proud to present the first major retrospective exhibition of paintings by 19th century American artist John George Brown. Revered in his lifetime for his sympathetic representation of children in both city and country, Brown projected a wholesome, optimistic vision to which his patrons readily responded. This exhibition clarifies the development of Brown's style and themes over the span of a long and distinguished career.

It is especially fitting that this exhibition be held here at the Smith Art Museum. A friend and patron of the artist, George Walter Vincent Smith bought and sold numerous Brown works at the height of his collecting in the late 19th century. Today his museum owns six Browns, the largest public collection of the artist's paintings. Correspondence between Smith and Brown indicates that Smith drove a hard bargain. Commenting on Smith's recent purchase, Brown wrote, "I would rather not send a bill, as I would not like it ever to be known I sold them at the price, as I do not think any other man could have got them, for we have very few men who have taken the interest in our native art that you have." Smith was also instrumental in the success of Springfield's Gill Gallery, where Brown showed some 70 paintings over his lifetime. Many of these works were purchased by Springfield area residents.

We are fortunate to have Martha Hoppin on our staff as curator. A scholar of 19th century American art, she organized the exhibition with care and discrimination. Her work is part of current scholarly inquiry to reevaluate the contribution of 19th century artists who have been neglected in this century. Other members of the museum staff participated in the realization of this project. Registrar Karen Papineau, assisted by Nancy Swallow and Heather Haskell, deftly handled the many complicated shipping arrangements; financial officer Terry Strozzi gracefully followed the twists and turns of the budget; David Stansbury cheerfully processed last-minute photograph orders, and preparator Bruce Rainier ably installed the exhibition. We owe special thanks to Debra Gorlin for her skill in editing the catalogue, to Deborah Hewitt, catalogue designer, for her patience in working with us, and to Diane Forsberg for her capable assistance with many aspects of the exhibition.

Finally, we are very appreciative of the support of our lenders, whose generosity in lending important works has contributed to this new review and assessment of J.G. Brown's work.

HOLLISTER STURGES, Director

George Walter Vincent Smith Art Museum/Museum of Fine Arts, Springfield

ACKNOWLEDGMENTS

I first began work on J.G. Brown at the suggestion of Richard Mühlberger, former director of the George Walter Vincent Smith Art Museum, whose support and encouragement were essential to my research. Over the several years of planning leading up to this exhibition, I benefitted greatly from the help and cooperation of many individuals. I would like to thank especially William H. Gerdts, City University of New York Graduate Center, and Merl M. Moore, Jr., National Museum of American Art, for so generously sharing their invaluable archival material on Brown. Other scholars kindly responded to my many questions. Chief among these I thank Gabriel Weisberg, University of Minnesota; Annette Blaugrund, New York; H. Barbara Weinberg, Queens College; Susan P. Casteras, Yale Center for British Art; David Nasaw, City University of New York, College of Staten Island; Barry O'Connell, Amherst College; and Daniel Czitrom, Mt. Holyoke College. Hollister Sturges, director of the George Walter Vincent Smith Art Museum, provided valuable advice at many stages of catalogue preparation. I also received assistance from Virginia White, David Patterson, and Lady Eden.

This exhibition could not have been organized without the willing cooperation of many art dealers. Though all were helpful, I am especially indebted to Deedee Wigmore of D. Wigmore Fine Art; David Henry of Spanierman Gallery; M.P. Naud of Hirschl and Adler Galleries; Bruce Chambers of Berry-Hill Galleries; Karen Acevedo of Alexander Gallery; Frederick Bernaski, Kennedy Galleries; and Renee Schwartz of Galleries Maurice Sternberg. In addition, Debra Force and Jay Cantor of Christie's deserve special thanks.

Brown's production was so extensive that I visited or contacted most museums in the country in the course of my research. Everywhere I met with help and encouragement. I am particularly grateful to Abigail Booth Gerdts, National Academy of Design; Sally Mills and Marc Simpson, Fine Art Museums of San Francisco; Linda Ferber and Barbara Gallati, The Brooklyn Museum; Diana Stradzes, Carnegie Museum; Lindsay Errington, National Gallery of Scotland; Jane Vickers, Tyne and Wear Museums Service; John Nice, Edinburgh College of Art; Peter G. Vasey, Scottish Record Office; Phyllis Peet, High Museum of Art; Betty Muirden and staff, Research Library, Yale Center for British Art; and Richard Ressmeyer, Brockton Art Museum.

Over 40 percent of the works in this exhibition come from private collectors, who are as passionate today about Brown's work as their 19th century counterparts were. I would like to express my deep gratitude to these collectors for their courtesy and kindness, and especially for their willingness to part with treasured paintings for a long time. Without their participation no exhibition could properly represent the artist.

MARTHA J. HOPPIN
Curator of American Art

Country Paths and City Sidewalks: The Art of J.G. Brown

Although few people outside of collectors and art historians know his name today, John George Brown was one of the most popular American artists of the late 19th century. As one contemporary critic observed, "We have no more popular artist in America than J.G. Brown. He is more certain of his audience, and more direct in his appeal to it, than any other."[1] His genre scenes of New York City street children were so widely reproduced that he copyrighted a great many of them. By the time he died a wealthy man in 1913, he must have painted about one thousand pictures.

A decade before his death Brown credited his success to an art grounded in the people. "I stand today where I did forty years ago. I believe in the people and consider it enough for one man's life work to interpret what the people like."[2] The people liked images of children, and so, like other American genre painters, Brown made childhood his primary subject. On one level, winsome children appealed to an audience that appreciated sentiment. On another level, children symbolized America's lost, innocent past and her hope for the future. Responsive to popular values, Brown reflected popular taste in his images. His roots were in sentimental English Victorian art and in the craft tradition of glass-making; his sensibility and his sources lay in popular culture. He painted types of American life, especially in his characterization of urban street children, and these types were readily identifiable, like stock figures in popular literature and theater. He represented both city and country children during the same years, moving effortlessly back and forth, doing one and then the other. His location partly determined his subjects; in winter he painted city scenes and in summer, country scenes. But there is also little break in the images themselves. The street boys are poor and ragged, but they share the same carefree, irrepressible spirit as country children. Brown's images express the deep longing for continuity between city and country characteristic of his time.

As a person Brown was methodical and without pretension, a man of routines. Contemporaries consistently noted his cheerful, direct manner. "A plain name, and a plain but earnest man, with no nonsense about him. A type of the good old-fashioned artist we read of in English novels: fond of his craft, fond of his pipe, fond of work, fond of good-fellowship."[3] Others picked out "warm-hearted generosity,... abounding perserverance,... and loyalty to friends."[4] He was the sort of artist who went to the studio every day, arriving punctually, and moved to the countryside in summer on a predictable schedule. He regarded painting as a profession rather than a high calling and furnished his studio in a practical manner, as a work-place, not an exotic setting. He relished routine and convention, and took pleasure in his craft. Voicing strong, mostly conservative, opinions on the subject of art, he praised European academic artists like Jules Breton, Jean-Léon Gérôme, and Ludwig Knaus but could not comprehend the unconventional art of Camille Corot. "I can't understand how an intelligent being can paint clearly the windows in a house across a river, and then make the trees on this side of the same river look like smoke."[5] Among American artists he admired Winslow Homer, Seymour Guy, and Worthington Whittredge, all men for whom he felt a sense of personal loyalty.

Brown was also a shrewd businessman who carefully built up his career by joining organizations, sending to exhibitions, meeting fellow artists, and copyrighting his paintings. Popular magazines like *Harper's Weekly* and *Harper's Young People* regularly reproduced his works (fig. 1). One of the most visible artists of his time, he contributed to all the major exhibitions in New York, including those held by the National Academy of Design, the Brooklyn Art Association, the American Watercolor Society, the Century Club, and the Artists' Fund Society, as well as to a number of commercial galleries. Rarely in the 1870's did he not have a painting on view somewhere in New York, and he exhibited also in many other American cities like St. Louis, Cincinnati, San Francisco, Detroit, Buffalo, Boston, and Philadelphia. With so many paintings coming and going from his studio, he may have needed a business agent. Reportedly, Brown amassed quite a fortune in real estate investments by the end of his life.[6] Furthermore, his art was limited partially by choice. He could have made his career as a portrait or landscape painter, but he found his niche in genre scenes of children, and he embraced the popular support that came to him as a result.

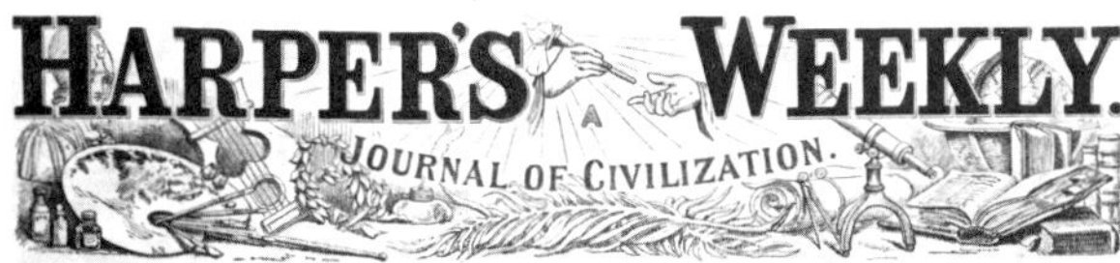
HARPER'S WEEKLY.
A JOURNAL OF CIVILIZATION.
NEW YORK, SATURDAY, APRIL 28, 1883.

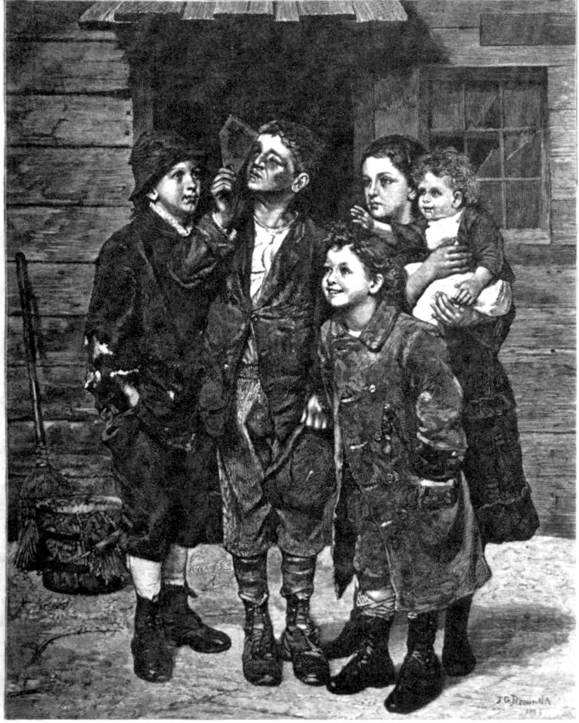

1. **Harper's Weekly** cover, April 28, 1883, Amherst College Library

Early Years

John George Brown, or "J.G." as he called himself, was born near Durham, England, on November 11, 1831. His parents, who were against his idea of becoming an artist, apprenticed him at age fourteen to a glass worker in Newcastle-on-Tyne. During his apprenticeship Brown enrolled in the evening drawing classes taught by William Bell Scott at the Government School of Design in Newcastle. Associated with the Pre-Raphaelite painters, Scott may have introduced his pupils to the intricate detail and glowing colors of Pre-Raphaelite art.

In 1852, at the age of twenty-one, Brown left Newcastle for Edinburgh. There he took a job in the Holyrood Glass Works by day and studied art at night at the Trustees Academy. Scott himself had studied at the Trustees Academy and may have influenced Brown to go there. Brown enrolled only in the antique class of the drawing department, which was taught by the Academy's director, Robert Scott Lauder. Lauder's novel approach to drawing from casts distinguished his teaching from that offered at other drawing schools. Students worked carefully and diligently on renderings of casts from ancient and Renaissance sculpture, but Lauder grouped the casts in striking and original ways and stressed the effect of the whole grouping, with its overall patterns of light and dark, as most important.[7] Brown must have learned well; at the end of the year he won a second prize in the annual competition of drawing from the antique. He was always very proud of his achievement and later recalled,

> While working, I was sent for from the Academy. This meant something to me, and I told one of my fellow-workmen that if I received a prize I would throw up my cap as I came in at the door of the long workshop. I was the lucky one, and, on arriving at the glass-house, I gave the promised signal, and the workshop rang with three cheers for the English boy who could work all day at his trade, and yet take a prize over the heads of those who gave their undivided attention to drawing.[8]

Brown emphasized here his diligence, the supportive comraderie of the workplace, and above all, his working-class origins. Throughout his career he liked to ally himself with the working class. "I began as a working-man,"[9] he said later, and in a somewhat self-serving manner always claimed a special sympathy with his working-class subjects.

Turning down a chance to study privately with Lauder, at the end of his year at the Trustees Academy Brown left Edinburgh for London, where he apparently tried painting portraits but worked primarily at designing for glass engravers. After three months in London, Brown emigrated to the United States.

It is difficult to establish the immediate effect of these years of training in England, since no student work by Brown is known to survive. None of his paintings, from his early years in New York or his career as a whole, suggests an interest in the historical or religious themes, or the Venetian color tradition, that preoccupied Robert Scott Lauder. Neither of his teachers even painted contemporary genre. For Brown his academic training in drawing and exposure to the general currents of English painting at mid-century were more critical influences. Rather than following the individual painting styles of his teachers, his earliest paintings grow directly from sentimental, illustrative Victorian genre painting.

Brown arrived in New York on his twenty-second birthday, settling first in Brooklyn, where he soon found employment at the Brooklyn Flint Glass Company.[10] His first months in this country proved successful. "Why, in the first week I earned four and twenty dollars. My board and lodging only ate up seven, and my washing—well, that ran up to three dollars fifty cents. This left me fourteen dollars clear. I had never seen such a sum before!"[11] In his spare time he continued to pursue his career as an artist. He attended classes at the newly opened Graham Art School, the first free art school in Brooklyn.[12] He also listed himself as a portrait painter in the 1855 Brooklyn city directory, but no portraits can be dated that early.

In September, 1855, Brown married Mary Owen, daughter of his employer, William Owen, co-owner of the Brooklyn Flint Glass Company. By all accounts, his father-in-law encouraged and probably supported him financially, making it possible for Brown to leave the glass works and turn to painting full time. By the next spring he was living with his wife's parents but had taken a studio in Brooklyn. There he began by painting portraits, as he said, "for anything I could get."[13] In 1856 William Owen died in the yellow fever epidemic, and the next year the Brooklyn Glass Company failed as a result of the great financial Panic of 1857, which caused bank closings, bankruptcies, and widespread unemployment. As he told an interviewer years later, since Owen's estate was lost, he supported the family by painting not only portraits but also "little pictures of children."[14] By 1860 Brown's genre paintings had caught on. While he continued to paint portraits on occasion through the rest of his career, he rarely exhibited one after this date.

Since Brown did not return to the glass factory, his financial situation could not have been dire. Instead, with a canny, methodical sureness, he took every necessary step to build his artistic career. He enrolled in 1857 in the National Academy of Design antique and life classes taught by Thomas Seir Cummings and continued in the life class there the next year. He launched his long and impressive exhibition record by sending two paintings to the National Academy of Design annual exhibition of 1858. In addition to making this foray from Brooklyn into the New York art world, Brown increased his involvement in the Brooklyn art community, becoming a founding member in 1859 of the Brooklyn Art Social and two years later of its successor, the Brooklyn Art Association.[15] He continued to show his work regularly at the Brooklyn Art Association and the National Academy of Design.

Active in all the major Brooklyn art organizations, Brown formed important friendships with other artists and potential patrons.[16] Presumably Brown first met prominent art dealer Samuel P. Avery in the late 1850's, when Avery was still active as an engraver but was already buying paintings from New York artists and hosting evening "Art Gatherings" in his Brooklyn home. Avery was instrumental in launching Brown's career as a genre painter, according to most contemporary accounts. Brown reportedly began selling his genre scenes of children for small sums in about 1858 or 1859. These attracted Avery, who "was among the first to buy, and on the strength of which he one evening invited Brown to his house to meet the artists of New York."[17] Avery most likely encouraged Brown to paint genre subjects, introduced him to New York artists, and helped him move in the summer of 1860 to a studio in New York's Tenth Street studio building.

Brown's move to the Tenth Street studio at this early point marks one of the milestones in his career, since almost all the prominent artists of his day were to establish studios there in the next two decades. Recently opened in 1858, the building soon became one of the focal points of artistic life in the city. Brown occupied this studio for the next fifty-three years, making him one of the longest-term tenants in the building's history. He continued to live in Brooklyn, however, for several more years and only took up permanent residence in New York City after about 1869. Between about 1863 and 1869 he resided in New Jersey, most likely in Fort Lee.[18] Thus he commuted to his studio from the country during the years he developed his characteristic image of both city and country children.

From the beginning Brown's genre scenes almost invariably depicted children. His children usually play outdoors, engaging in typical pastimes like flying kites, gathering flowers, throwing snowballs, going to school, playing dress-up, and playing soldier. Most of the works are humorous and light-hearted. While he painted a few scenes of children in the city during the 1860's, country children comprised the majority of his subjects until as late as 1875.

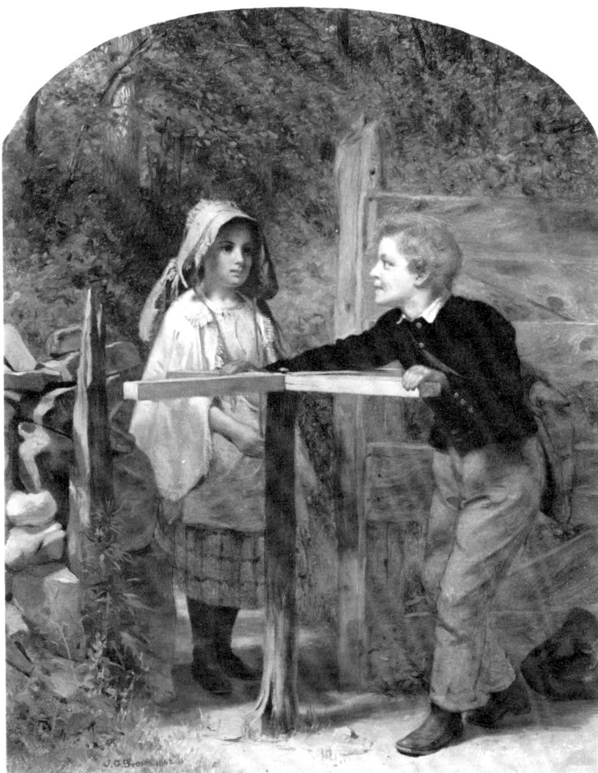

2. **Pay Toll,** 1862, Private Collection

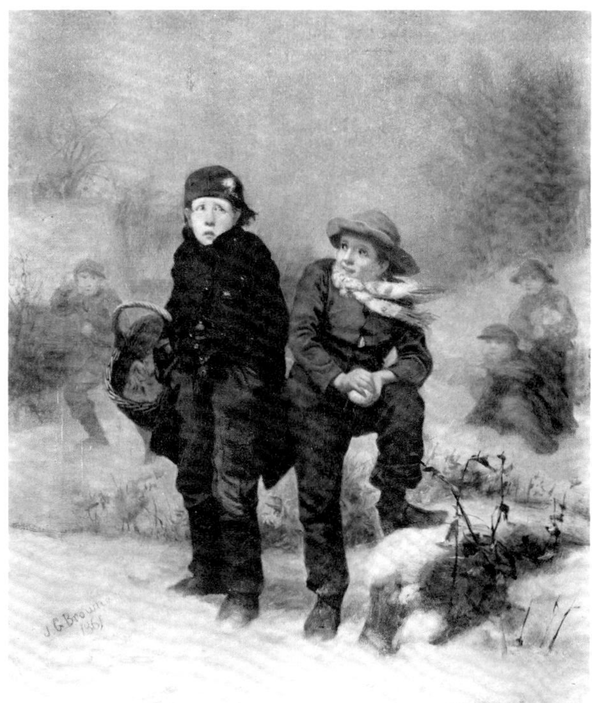

3. **The Victim,** 1861, National Academy of Design, New York

Of particular interest for their novelty in American art are his many early works which explore the theme of children imitating adult activities, particularly courtship rituals. Brown selected these subjects for their humor, rather than their potential for satire. In *Pay Toll*, for example, a work dated 1862 (fig. 2), a young boy demands a toll from a young girl about to enter the turnstile gate of a rustic fence. Clearly, the act parallels adult flirtation. The typical age of Brown's young lovers ranged from about eight to twelve years old, but could go as low as six. Although most of these subjects date from the early 1860's, Brown continued to treat the theme of young love through that decade and the next, indicating the ongoing popularity of such scenes.

In style and subject Brown's early genre scenes are most like conventional, sentimental English scenes of childhood that had great popular appeal. Works by William Mulready, a follower of David Wilkie in the early 19th century, and by Mulready's followers, notably Thomas Webster, probably influenced him most. Mulready was particularly noted for introducing one of the most popular Victorian subjects, the mischievous boy, a type Brown was to paint throughout his career.[19] *The Victim*, painted by Brown in 1861 (fig. 3), is reminiscent of Mulready's interpretation of childhood.

Particularly in his paintings of youthful courtship Brown looked to English example. In *Pay Toll* Brown followed English conventions for portraying adult courtship when he placed the boy and girl on either side of a country stile.[20] While young courting couples appear in works by English artist William Maw Egley, they can be found more readily in English popular illustration.[21] In the pages of *Punch* magazine, young boys and girls flirt and kiss in situations that poke fun at adult behavior and at social customs of Victorian upper-class children. Widely known and available in America, *Punch* could have provided Brown with a popular source for his imagery.

In *The Victim* and *Pay Toll* Brown drew as well on American genre traditions in forming his compositions, figural types, and facial expressions. Humor and anecdote were fundamental to American genre painting, which had its roots in the English art of David Wilkie and 17th century Dutch art. William Sidney Mount, founder of an American genre school in the 1830's and 1840's, often depicted young, sometimes mischievous boys playing in outdoor settings. Certainly Brown borrowed occasional figural types and

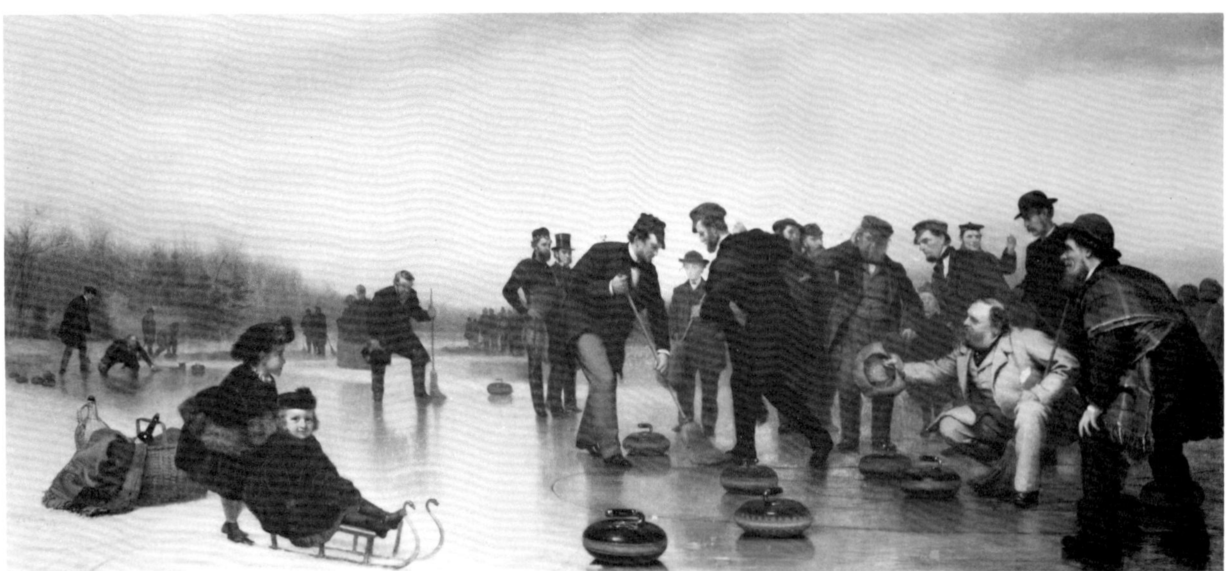

4. **Curling;—a Scottish Game, at Central Park,** 1863, Lady Eden, daughter of Robert Gordon, whose great-uncle, Robert Gordon, is featured in the painting (not in exhibition)

expressions from Mount, as in the smiling boy in *The Victim*. The careful geometric structure of *Pay Toll* probably also derives from Mount's example. Although Brown's later work showed the influence of Eastman Johnson, who assumed leadership of the American genre field by about 1860, at this early stage Brown remained closer to the older tradition of William Sidney Mount.

Brown's career continued to follow a direct and deliberate course. An associate member in 1861 of the prestigious National Academy of Design, as if on schedule he was elected to full membership in 1863. Thus began a long period of association with the Academy, during which Brown served as council-member, visiting instructor (1875), and finally vice-president from 1899 to 1903. According to contemporary accounts, his election was based on a highly acclaimed group portrait painted in 1863. Commissioned by prominent Scottish businessman Robert Gordon, *Curling:—a Scottish Game, at Central Park* (fig. 4) represents members of the St. Andrew's Curling Club on the ice during a curling match. Why Gordon selected Brown as the artist is not known; it may not have been an artistic connection (Gordon was a noted art collector) but simply the lucky fact of Brown's British birth.

The success of this work no doubt led to a second group portrait, *Claiming the Shot: After the Hunt in the Adirondacks*, painted in 1865 for William Brand, one of the men depicted in *Curling at Central Park* (fig. 5). Along with Gordon, Brand had been a founder of the curling club; also like Gordon, Brand was of Scottish birth and returned home not long after commissioning the painting. For many years it has been assumed that Brown's portrait represented members of the famous Astor family, but this now seems doubtful. The portly central figure, once thought to be John Jacob Astor III, is more likely William Brand, and the other men probably members of a hunting club.

In *Claiming the Shot*, as opposed to *Curling at Central Park*, a mood of concentration and quiet reflection prevails. Against a colorful forest background the central group of men stands out in strong relief, their faces and forms evenly lit and meticulously painted. Though Brown fastidiously plotted the arrangement of the central group to provide variety of pose yet maintain unity, the effect is informal and relaxed. The men are in all stages of standing and sitting, and all participate naturally in the discussion. The result is a seemingly unposed conversation piece. Despite the artistic success of these two large portraits, no other groups like them are known.

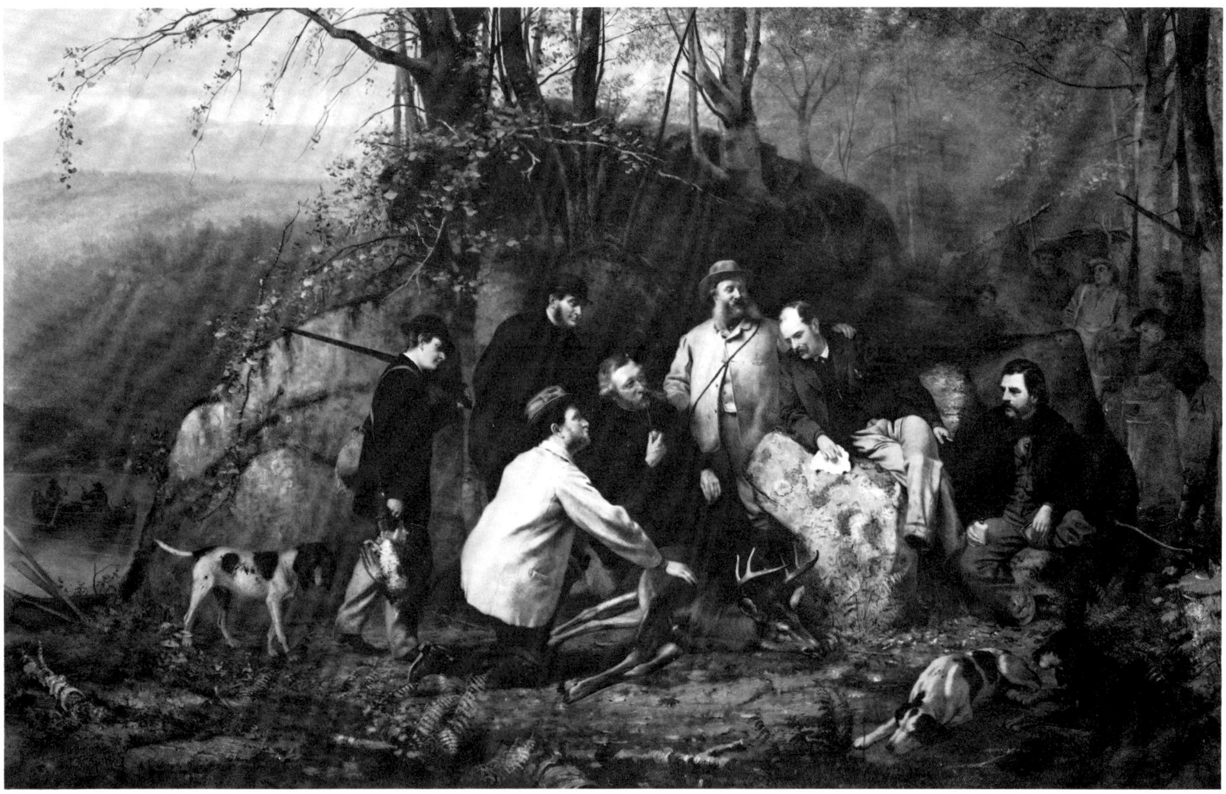

5. **Claiming the Shot: After the Hunt in the Adirondacks,** 1865, The Detroit Institute of Arts, Founders Society Purchase, Robert H. Tannahill Foundation Fund

The two group portraits, and especially the second of 1865, mark an advance in realism compared to Brown's earlier genre scenes. After about 1864 he paid careful attention to detail, rendered volume and spatial effects more convincingly, and relied on light to unify his compositions. In *Silver Birches* of 1864 (fig. 48), he very specifically treated a magnificent birch tree trunk, showing every curl and twist of the peeling bark with its various textures and patterns. This change to a highly developed and exacting realism is most apparent, however, in *Resting in the Woods*, a painting from 1866 (fig. 34). By this date he painted every part of the picture with equal detail, whereas in earlier works, he usually thinly and loosely brushed in backgrounds, as in *Silver Birches*. By the time he painted *Resting in the Woods*, Brown had also fully realized his interest in dappling effects of outdoor sunlight.

Pre-Raphaelite Influence

Brown's mature realism, particularly his new emphasis on accurate recording and descriptive detail, most likely stemmed from contact with American Pre-Raphaelite painters, who were most active in the mid-1860's. Under the influence of English critic John Ruskin, a number of Americans worked in a highly detailed, polished realist style that featured close-up views of small segments of nature. In focusing on the bark of one birch tree, Brown emulated the American Pre-Raphaelites, whose favorite subjects included tree trunks, leaves, and grasses.[22]

Brown knew at least one of the American Pre-Raphaelites, Charles Herbert Moore, and probably was acquainted with several others, who included Thomas C. Farrer, John William Hill, his son John Henry Hill, and William Trost Richards. Moore had a studio in the Tenth Street building from 1859 to 1861, where Brown may first have met him. In 1864 Moore and Brown exhibited their collaborative work, titled *The Spring* (location unknown), in which Moore painted the landscape and Brown the figures.[23]

Through his participation in the American Watercolor Society, which began meeting in 1866, Brown had additional exposure to Ruskin's American followers. He was one of the earliest members of the Society, joining in 1867 alongside Farrer and Moore. Although Brown did not contribute to the society's annual exhibitions until 1872, he later served as its president from 1887 to 1904.

The paintings which best exemplify Brown's Pre-Raphaelite style date from 1865 and 1866 and treat almost the same subject, a young girl in a forest interior. *The Little Queen of the Woods*, dated 1865, and *Resting in the Woods*, dated 1866 (figs. 6 and 34), both feature detailed study of foreground leaves and grasses. Dense forest growth and large boulders limit any view into the distance, or any real middle-ground, and direct attention to the figure and the textures and surface variety of rock, bark, moss, and leaf. Brown also closely observed the girls' clothing, paying particular attention to such details as hats and shoes.

Brown was fascinated with the effect of small patches of sunlight sprinkled over a leafy, shaded forest interior and explored this contrast of sunlight and shadow through the rest of his career. Possibly he was inspired by the work of American Pre-Raphaelite William Trost Richards, who painted a number of landscapes in the late 1850's and early 1860's which feature wooded glades dappled with sunshine. In Brown's paintings light strikes selected parts of the figures and the foliage, creating an animated pattern. Rarely, however, does light fall directly on his figures' faces; as in *Resting in the Woods*, it usually outlines the head from behind. This kind of backlighting became Brown's standard treatment, enabling him to model form and describe features fully without sacrificing detail.

Brown characteristically developed his subjects in clusters, painting compositionally and thematically related scenes within a few years of each other. The "girl-with-tree" forms one such theme and variation series painted in the mid-60's. The motif of the large tree trunk may derive from English Pre-Raphaelite works by John Everett Millais and Arthur Hughes, who painted several well-known compositions placing women next to large foreground trees. In Brown's art this subject, along with its variant of a young girl peeking out from behind foliage, allowed him to limit the background, focus on detail of figure and foreground setting, and create an image of emerging womanhood.

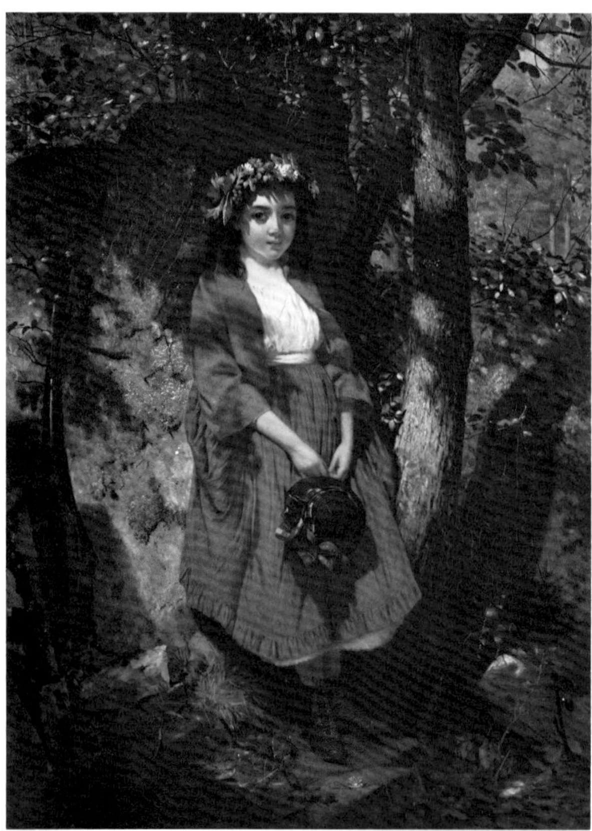

6. **The Little Queen of the Woods,** 1865, The Jones Library, Inc., Amherst, Mass.

Within the same compositional type he varied the expression of each work. The young girl in *The Little Queen of the Woods* gazes boldly, even provocatively, at the viewer. In *Thus Perish the Memory of Our Love* of 1865 (fig. 7) a beautiful, young woman dreamily peels the bark from a splendid birch trunk. The many similarities of *Watching the Woodpecker*, dated 1866 (fig. 36), to *Resting in the Woods* make the two works seem like companion pieces. Almost exactly the same size, they present complementary times of day and a similarly meditative mood. *Watching the Woodpecker*, however, treats the broader theme of the transience of life through the sunset and the enormous tree trunk which has been hacked with an ax.[24]

Though the late sixties were not as cohesive or productive a period as the middle of the decade, they do hold some important developments in Brown's artistic and personal life. In these years he began to reach a more popular audience through the reproduction of his works. Between 1868 and 1870 six compositions were issued as chromolithographs, five of these by the leading firm of Louis Prang and Company.[25] In spite of Eastman's Johnson's greater critical acclaim, in 1870 Prang offered more works after Brown than any other genre painter. Four of Brown's chromos were country scenes of young girls playing outdoors.

In 1867 Brown's wife died, leaving him with two young daughters, aged about six and three. At first he remained in Fort Lee, New Jersey, where the family had probably been living since about 1863, but by 1869 he had moved his permanent residence to New York City. When he married again in July 1871, it was to his sister-in-law, Emma Augusta Owen, who was then only eighteen.

Quite possibly Brown's increased interest in compositions involving young women, rather than little girls, reflected his own courtship. In the late 1860's he painted several idealized young women, including the literary heroine Maud Muller in a lost composition known only from a chromolithograph. In 1870 he executed at least three genre scenes of women. One of these is the well-known *Music Lesson* (fig. 8), which represents a young couple playing a flute in a middle-class parlor.[26] The principal subject is courtship, not music, and their shared flute serves as an excuse for the meeting. The well-appointed interior contains a heavy, carved Renaissance Revival sofa and numerous other examples of contemporary Victorian taste. An elaborate plant stand, patterned carpets and wallpaper, heavy draperies, ornate harp, and numerous pictures fill the small, narrow corner of the room. This kind of interior, with its use of works of art to expand or reinforce the narrative of the painting, resembles settings found in English Pre-Raphaelite paintings, especially those by Millais, Holman Hunt, and James Collinson.[27] In Brown's *Music Lesson* the prints in the background depict couples and are arranged in pairs. Unlike English Pre-Raphaelite examples, however, Brown's painting has no underlying moral; the couple just enjoy the flirtation. Brown occasionally painted adult couples, rather than children; what is more unusual here is the middle-class, interior setting.

A similar setting and the same harp appear in another painting from 1870, a work now titled *The Harpist* but originally known as *"A Sweet Singer in Israel"* (fig. 27). This title derives from a phrase used to describe the Biblical King David, who played the harp and was noted as a psalm writer. Whether the painting portrays an actual singer or concert is unknown, but the entire conception is

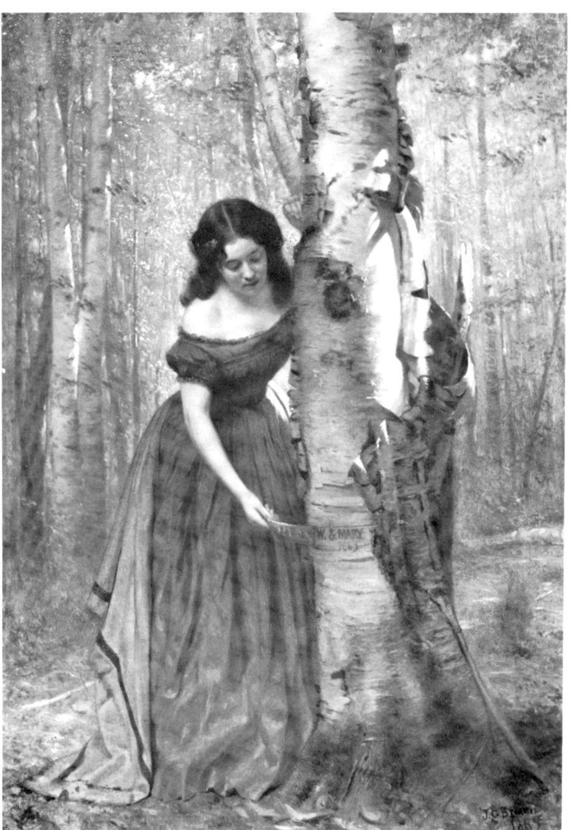

7. **Thus Perish the Memory of Our Love,** 1865, Edward and Deborah Pollack Fine Art, New York (not in exhibition)

unusual for Brown and may have been a commissioned portrait.

After completing these two interior scenes, in late summer Brown sailed for Europe in the company of New York dealer John Snedecor, who regularly sold Brown's paintings.[28] Apparently his first trip abroad since he had immigrated seventeen years ago, it lasted only about six weeks. He visited Scotland and England, where he reported being most impressed with Turner's landscapes. A two-week stay in France was cut short by advancing Prussians. The trip had no immediate effect on Brown's art, however, and his paintings showed no change in style or subject following his return. Except for a possible visit to England in 1885, he remained in America for the rest of his career. Believing that American artists should only go abroad for their training after developing "an individuality of their own," he advised them to come home and paint American subjects, as he did.[29]

In the 1870's Brown's career reached its height. During these years his paintings were most consistently well conceived, well executed,

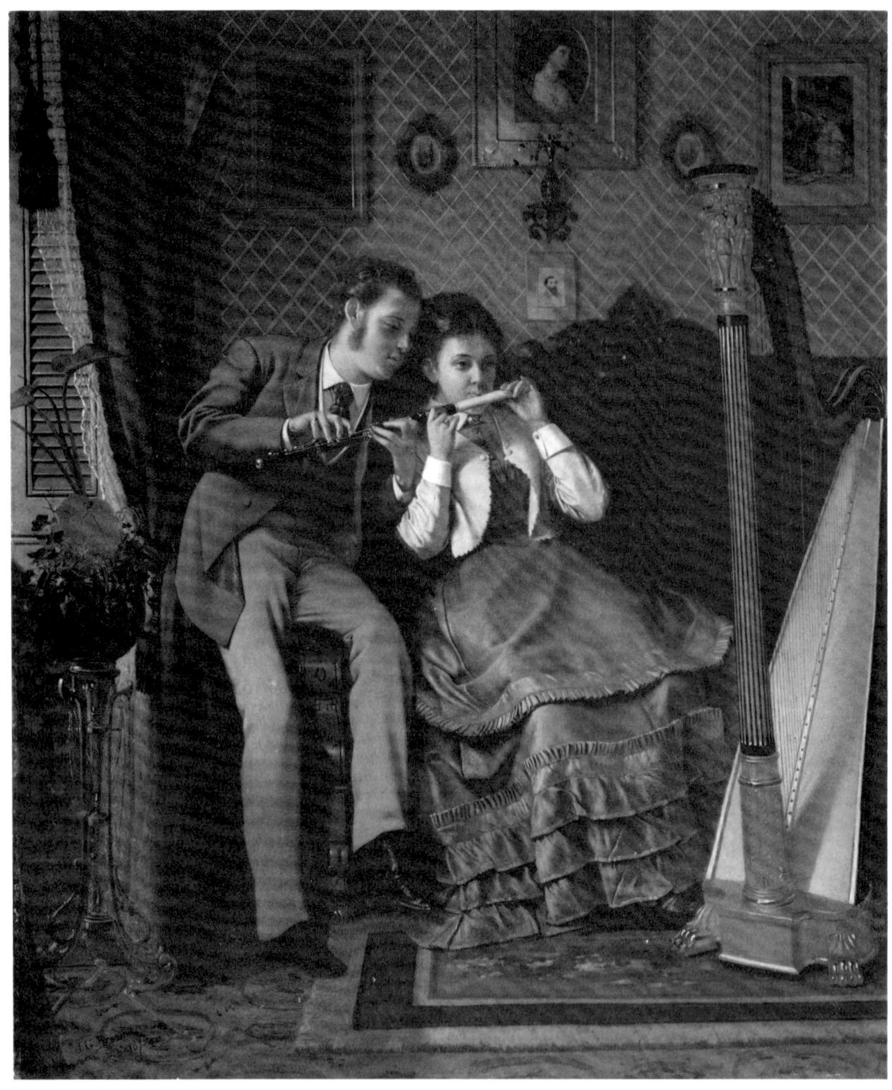

8. **The Music Lesson,** 1870, Lent by The Metropolitan Museum of Art; Gift of Colonel Charles A. Fowler, 1921

and well reviewed. In terms of style, in the 1870's Brown synthesized earlier Pre-Raphaelite handling and interest in landscape features with a broader treatment of light and brushwork. The works of the mid-70's are polished and detailed, but without the painstaking realism of the mid-60's. Gradually during the 1870's Brown's brushwork loosened somewhat, as part of the broad shift in style affecting most American painters under the influence of contemporary French art.

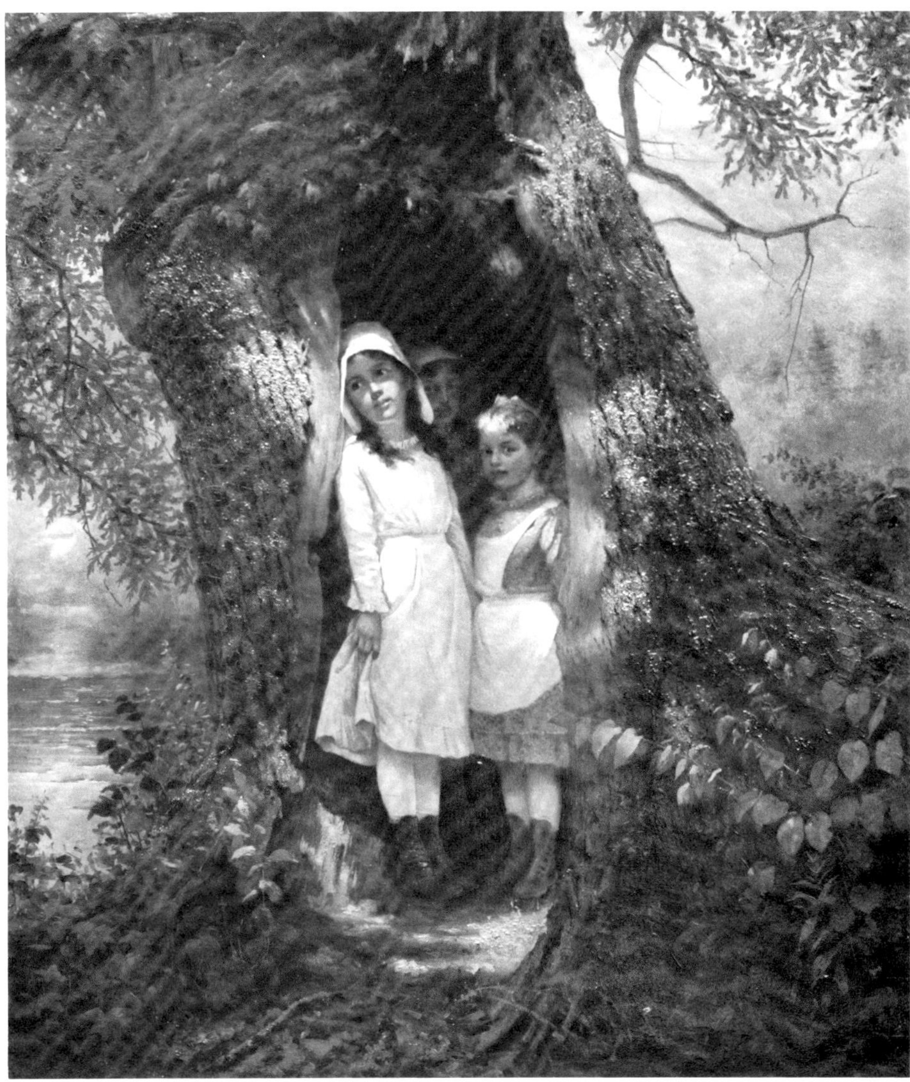

9. **Hiding in the Old Oak,** 1874, St. Johnsbury Athenaeum

Country Scenes

For the first half of the decade, Brown continued to paint country children. *Picnic Party in the Woods,* dated 1872 (fig. 33), painted the year before Brown plunged into city themes, summarizes the pleasures and virtues of country life enjoyed by a number of middle-class families. He particularly singled out a large group of children playing a familiar game called, "Oats, Peas, Beans."[30] The game's sung refrain, "waiting for a partner," signals the main theme of courtship. Brown echoed the young, spotlit couple playing the game by painting pairs of children and adults throughout the picture. Since he included all generations, from a tiny infant to an old man, the painting's broad subject is the traditional stages of life: childhood, adulthood, and old age.

Brown's evocations of idyllic country childhood culminated in three outstanding works from the mid-1870's which he exhibited at the National Academy of Design to wide acclaim. *Hiding in the Old Oak,* 1874 (fig. 9), *Gathering Autumn Leaves,* 1875 (fig. 10), and *The Country Gallants,* 1876 (fig. 26), all show children playing and exploring in nature, and all three rely on light, particularly Brown's favorite sun-dappled effects, to convey rustic beauty.

Brown began work on *Hiding in the Old Oak* in the summer of 1873.[31] By that time he had established his working pattern of summers spent in the country gathering material for rural subjects which he then executed in the studio

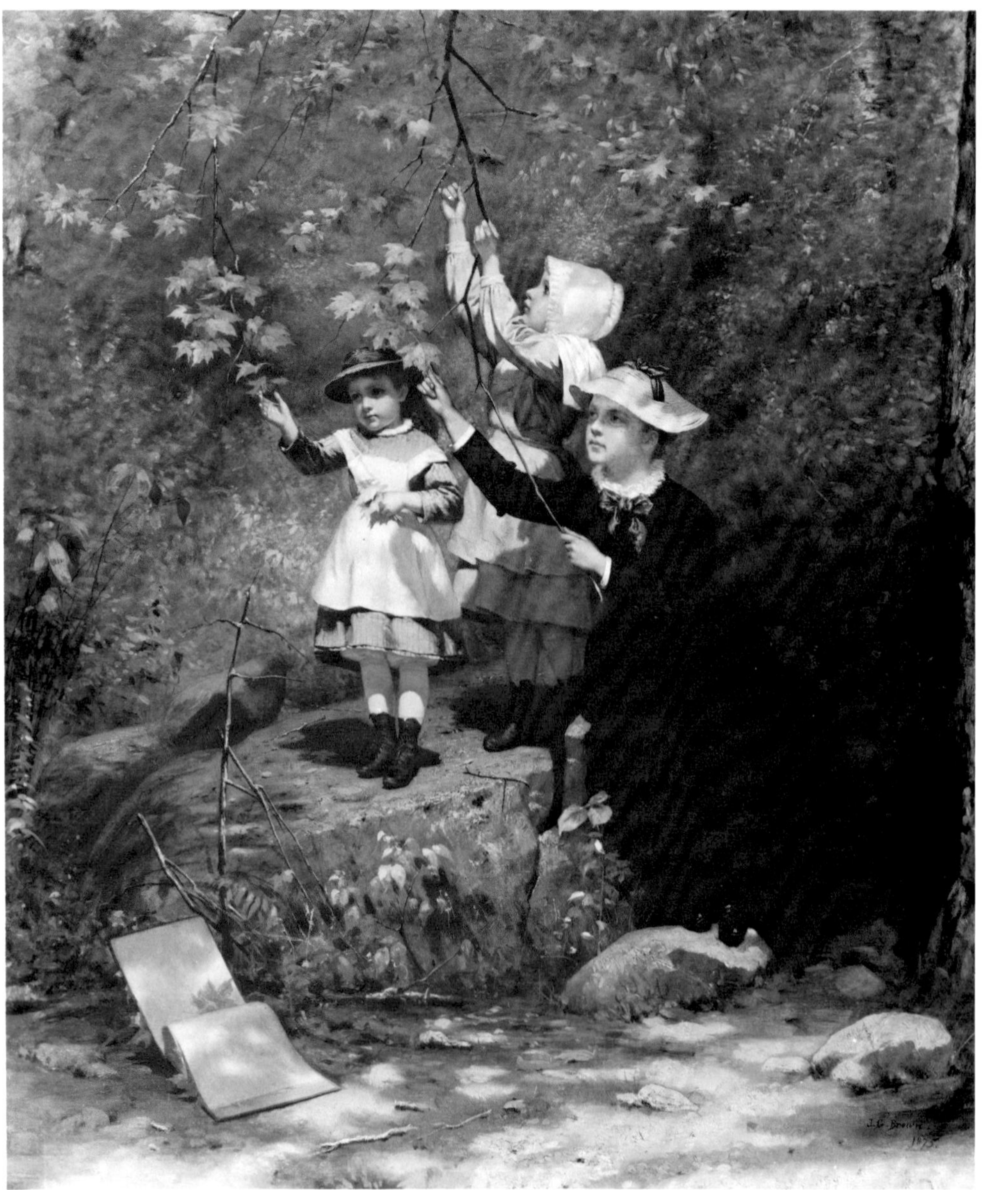

10. **Gathering Autumn Leaves,** 1875, Private Collection

over the fall and winter, usually showing the most important work at the next spring's Academy exhibition. He typically closed his Tenth Street studio in July and returned to the city in early October.

Hiding in the Old Oak successfully combines landscape and narrative. Three young girls hide in the hollow of an enormous tree trunk, presumably awaiting another playmate. Just enough of a story is told, or hinted at, to supply narrative interest. Brown evoked the love of outdoors, of adventure, of anticipation; part of the painting's appeal is the childhood memories it recalls. At the same time he painted a kind of cycle of life, juxtaposing the girls' youthfulness to the aged tree. While the pristine forest symbolizes the children's youth and innocence, it also sounds a note of underlying sensuality. The luxuriant, moist foliage and womb-like hollow tree contrast with the children's purity and innocence in a confusion of sensuality and spirituality not atypical of the Victorian era.

The composition and treatment of light in *Hiding in the Old Oak* recall Brown's earlier paintings of similar girl-and-tree subjects, such as *Resting in the Woods.* While detailed, *Hiding in the Old Oak* lacks the sharp precision and minuteness of Brown's Pre-Raphaelite style. Here, he more roughly and broadly executed the foliage, rendering the bark of the hollow oak, for example, with obvious brushstrokes and impasto.

Since they probably both stem from his 1873 summer trip to the Catskills, *Hiding in the Old Oak* and *Gathering Autumn Leaves,* completed in the spring of 1875,[32] may have been envisioned as complementary, one the epitome of lush summer, the other of vivid autumn. One painting depicts children playing alone, while in the other two young children gather fall leaves in the company of a well-dressed young woman. Rarely do adults intrude in Brown's country—or city—scenes. Here the woman, perhaps their mother, assumes the role of helper.

The fall setting gave Brown the chance to explore color as well as light. He sprinkled patches of light over the fore-and middle ground of the painting, creating a frothy, lacy effect also conveyed by the scattered, irregular maple leaves. Touches of bright color add more movement to the scene. Red and yellow leaves form a boldly colorful background, made even more vivid by the woman's black dress. The bright blue and yellow accents of bow, apron, and hat enliven the unusual color harmonies found in the children's lavender and peach costumes. Brown was sometimes capable of subtle and unorthodox color combinations. *Young Girl in a New York Garden* from 1871, for instance (cover illus.), is carefully structured through different planes of peach, tan, and pink. Often, as in *Gathering Autumn Leaves,* he combined frosty pink, lavender, and peach, with bright red or blue touches.

The third of Brown's great country scenes of the mid-70's, *The Country Gallants* of 1876 (fig. 26), best demonstrates his new ability to integrate figures in a landscape. During this decade, in fact, he made pure landscape studies on his summer excursions, which resulted in a greater variety and expanded role of landscape settings in his paintings.

Brown had painted landscapes as early as 1861, when he offered for sale a *Sunrise, from the Palisades,* and he exhibited landscapes sporadically after that time.[33] Since few of his landscapes are known today, it is difficult to generalize on his landscape style and themes. Yet they seem to have paralleled the development of his genre paintings in moving from a Pre-Raphaelite exactness in the mid-60's to a more informal, though still highly realistic, technique in the mid-70's. With some exceptions, he favored forest interiors during both decades, as he did in his genre scenes.

Clearly, given his outstanding painting from 1867, the large-scale *View of the Palisades, Hudson River* (fig. 35), Brown could have pursued a career as a landscape painter had he chosen to. Brown painted his large, panoramic view of the cliffs of Fort Lee, New Jersey, as a background for river boat activity. His accurate portrait of a particular steamboat, as well as the large size of the landscape, were unusual for Brown at this time, and he probably executed this subject, as he did the two large group portraits, on commission.[34]

Brown sketched the landscape during his summer in the White Mountains in 1872, and he continued the practice into the mid-70's. He spent some time in the western Massachusetts town of Huntington during the summer of 1874. *Waterfall, Huntington, Massachusetts* (fig. 52) probably typifies the essential features of his landscapes: water coursing over stones, forest tree trunks, branches with varied foliage, scattered sunlight animating the whole. While he exhibited some of his landscapes, even sending one to the National Academy in 1875, most are now lost. The majority must have resembled this one, presumably painted on-the-spot and intended ultimately to strengthen the settings of his genre scenes. While reviewers of the 1875 Academy exhibition considered his landscape entry to be a promising new departure, he exhibited few landscapes after this time.

The Country Gallants benefitted from Brown's experiments with landscape. Clearly a genre painting rather than a landscape with incidental figures, the work is Brown's ultimate statement about children crossing a stream, a recurrent subject which he had often painted in the past (see, for example, fig. 38). The title refers to the gentlemanly manner of the two boys helping the girls across the stream. One girl has already reached the other side, but her companion steps gingerly as both boys take hold of her hands to steady her. While the subject may be Brown's favorite one of country courtship, his typical coyness and humorous flirting are absent. A combination of light, color, and brushwork creates an enchanting, pure, and tranquil world. By contrast to the meticulously described foreground, the background foliage becomes a soft, feathery mass of golden autumn color, providing a glowing core to the composition. The whole nostalgic scene celebrates rustic simplicity and the natural good manners of the country dweller.

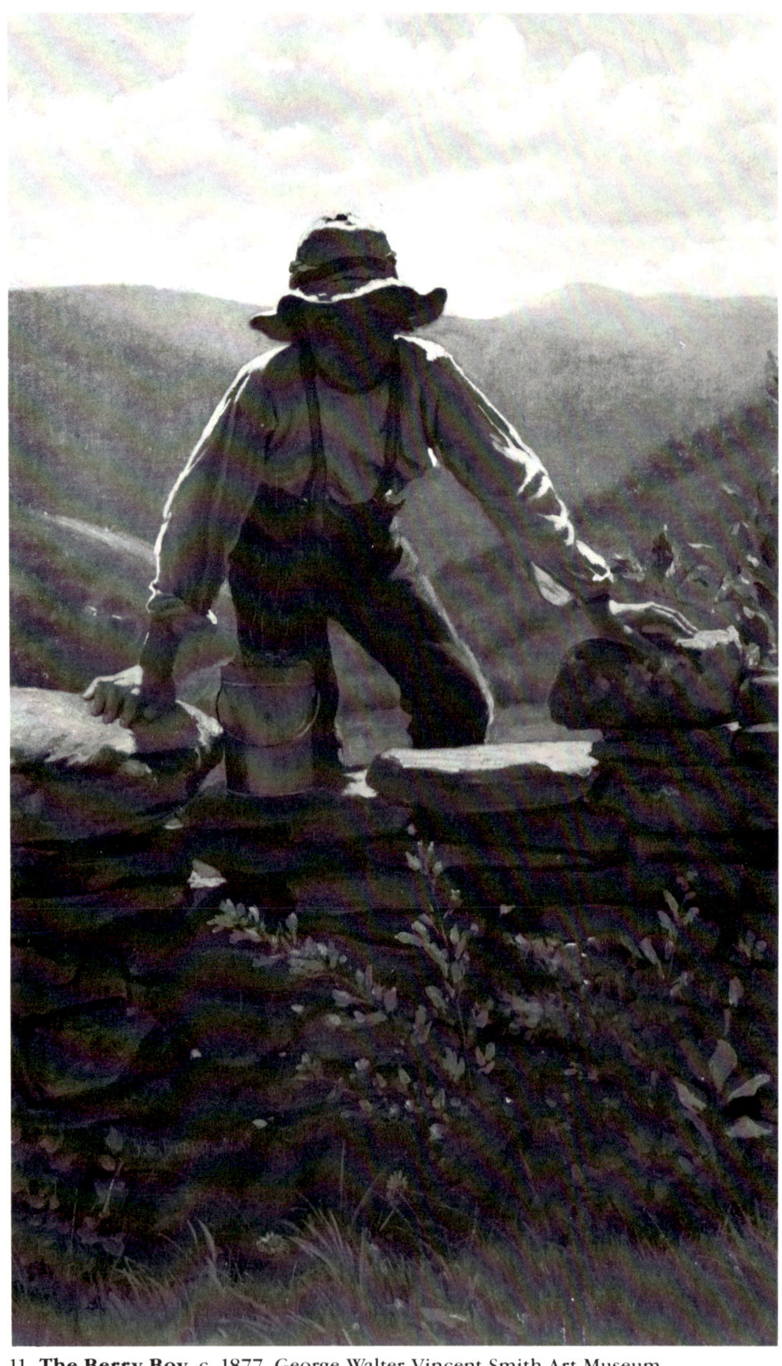

11. **The Berry Boy,** c. 1877, George Walter Vincent Smith Art Museum, Springfield, Massachusetts

Brown's Contemporaries

Like many of his contemporaries, Brown romantically envisioned country life, where the country boy embodied a lost golden age. *The Berry Boy* of about 1877 (fig. 11) epitomizes this carefree country existence. The young boy, pausing as he climbs over a stone fence, looks directly out at the viewer. His active pose and radiant face express the joy of being outdoors on a sunny day.

In depicting his country boys Brown drew from a well-established vocabulary which already existed by the mid-1870's. Based on William Sidney Mount's country boys of the 1840's,

Eastman Johnson further developed the type in the early 1860's and Winslow Homer refined it in the 1870's. Johnson's archetypal image, *The Barefoot Boy,* which Prang reproduced as a chromolithograph in 1867, codified the costume and expression of the country boy in painting and illustration. These essential features—bare feet, rolled up pants (sometimes held up by suspenders), a loose, white, long-sleeved shirt, rumpled (usually straw) hat, fresh face, and happy expression—came to visually define the country boy.[35] Brown borrowed from this tradition as well as contributed to its development.

Both Johnson and Homer undoubtedly influenced Brown's portrayal of country children in the 1870's. His choice of subjects in particular, and his idealization, followed their lead, but he remained distinct from them in many ways. First, whereas both Johnson and Brown remained strongly tied to narrative, Johnson explored a wider range of compositional schemes and subjects, including children indoors and out, with adults and without. Johnson also painted many more interiors. Homer, on the other hand, did not individualize his figures and played down narrative. Second, while all three artists explored the effects of strong, outdoor sunlight, Brown developed the sun-dappled forest interior as his characteristic setting. Finally, the majority of Brown's country scenes feature young girls, rather than boys. It was in his city subjects that Brown overwhelmingly portrayed young boys. Drawn to the more sentimental aspects of country girls as subjects, Brown may also have deliberately sought to develop his own specialty for both commercial and artistic reasons.

The Cider Mill of 1880 (fig. 25) is one of Brown's last great country scenes, a tour de force of patterned light and a collection of particularly appealing little girls. Like Homer and Johnson at the same time, Brown moved away from his bucolic views of country life at the beginning of the 1880's. Homer took up sea subjects; Johnson painted portraits. Brown turned almost exclusively to the city subjects he had painted increasingly since the mid-70's. He had depicted city street life sporadically up to this time, gradually building up a market for such scenes over ten years. With the popularity of his country scenes, he had little commercial incentive to change; probably a shift in patronage in the late 1870's, one that affected other artists as well, encouraged the production of city scenes. By the end of the decade Brown was firmly associated with the theme of the city boy urchin, especially the bootblack.

City Streets

As early as 1861 Brown exhibited a work titled *Only One Cent, Sir,* and in 1863 he showed a *Delivery Boy.*[36] Both probably portrayed city children working. In 1863 he painted *The Beggars* (fig. 12), which may represent his earliest rendition of newsboys and crossing sweepers, two prominent types of child workers found in the city streets. Two young crossing sweepers, a boy and a girl, joke with a colleague who pretends to pay them for their efforts. Presumably a newsboy, he carries one or more copies of the New York *Herald* under his arm. Despite the presence of a fourth figure, a sad boy who appears to be begging, the painting is lighthearted. This tone is in keeping with the rest of Brown's genre paintings from this period, which humorously present episodes from children's lives.

The representation of street merchants had a long history in English and French art, going back particularly to the 18th century "Cries," popular prints which portrayed all the different city vendors and the characteristic cries they used to advertise their wares. Fruit vendors and flower girls became especially favorite subjects in 19th century English art; before 1870 they were usually portrayed as attractive and appealing children.[37] Crossing sweepers, too, though not so numerous, entered English art well before 1860, and were presented in the same picturesque vein. The best known and most obvious example for Brown would have been the sweet, deferential boy in William Powell Frith's *Crossing Sweeper* (unlocated) of 1858. One could find characterizations closer to Brown's in the pages of *Punch* magazine, which in the 1840's and 1850's printed many humorous representations of dirty, disheveled crossing sweepers; often they enjoy some kind of boyish amusement.[38] French Realist painters of the 1850's chose subjects from city life, but they presented street merchants more soberly and sympathetically, sensitive to the harsh reality of their lives. Brown may have been entirely unaware of the French Realist movement; at least his interpretation of city street life in the 1860's followed English example.

American artists had begun to turn to street life for subject matter by the 1840's. These subjects increased in popularity in the next two decades but did not appear frequently until the 1870's and 1880's. Americans chose to paint street musicians, merchants, and beggars among the earliest types, since they were already established subjects in European art. Also predictably,

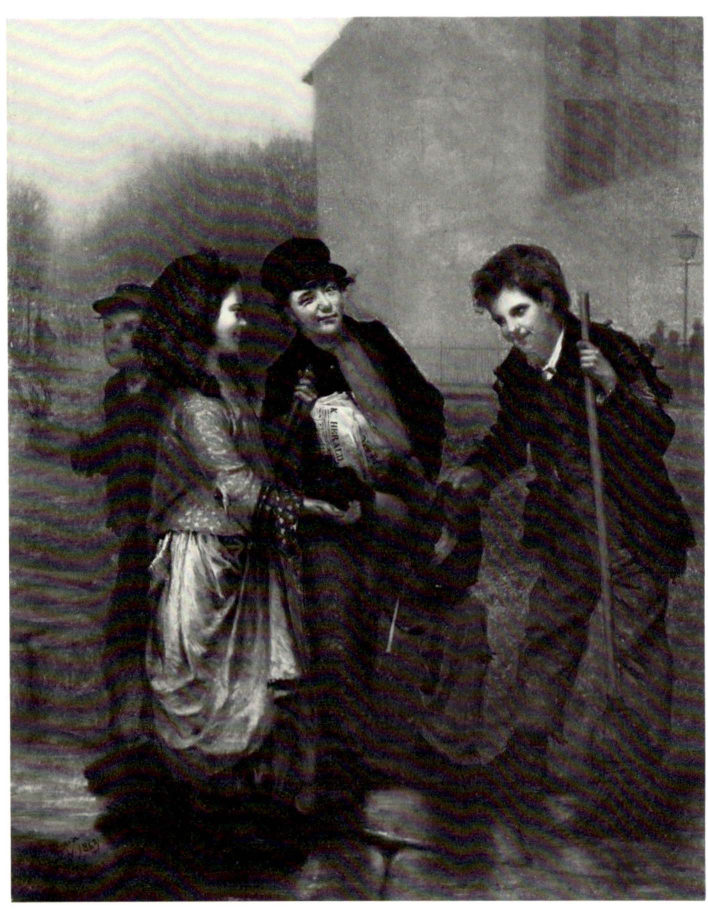

12. **The Beggars,** 1863, Wichita Art Museum, Wichita, Kansas

most artists who first depicted such themes were living, or had lived, in Europe. When the young George Flagg was in London in 1836, for example, he painted *The Match Girl* (New-York Historical Society), probably the earliest street waif by an American.[39] William Morris Hunt and Eastman Johnson also painted child street musicians, flower sellers, and chimney sweeps while living in France and The Hague in the early 1850's. Although some artists depicted adult street types, as in Thomas Waterman Wood's aged ragpicker, *La Chiffonnière* (Metropolitan Museum of Art), painted in Paris in 1859, for the most part these subjects were children.

While he hardly appeared in European painting, the newsboy was already an established figure in American genre painting by the 1860's, largely because the newspaper itself symbolized the glorious future of American democracy.[40] Not surprisingly, the city newsboy was painted mostly by American artists who had little tie to Europe. Henry Inman probably first captured him in his 1841 *Newsboy* (Addison Gallery of American Art),[41] possibly the source of Brown's background setting in *The Beggars.* Thomas Le Clear executed several versions of the newsboy beginning as early as 1845, and between 1857 and 1861 New York artist James Cafferty painted two newsboy pictures (private collection), as well as included two newsboys in his large view of Wall Street during the Panic of 1857 (Museum of the City of New York). Despite Brown's probable contact with both Le Clear and Cafferty, his earliest interpretation of the newsboy remains distinct from theirs in stressing humor and group comraderie. Although he continued to paint city children, Brown portrayed the newsboy only occasionally and mostly late in his career, after he had established himself as the painter of bootblacks.

With *The First Cigar* of 1863 (now lost), Brown inaugurated his long-standing association with ragamuffin city-boy subject matter.[42] His theme, the discomfort of one young smoker amid the bravado of his more experienced companions (one of whom blows smoke in his face), was intentionally humorous. The painting gained

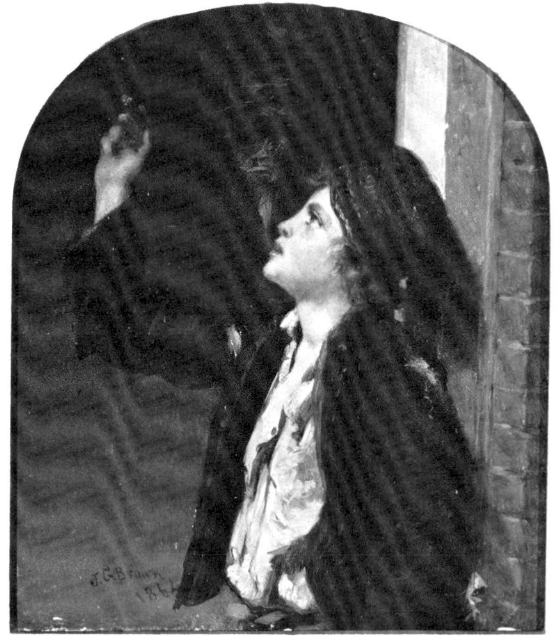
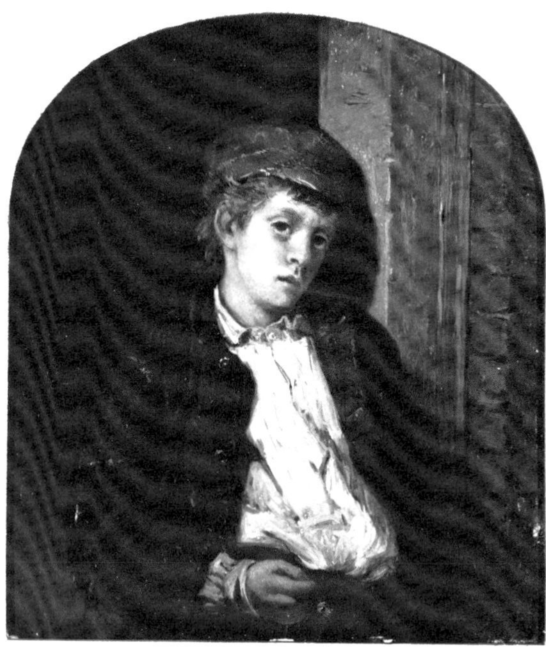

13. **Allegro** and **Penseroso,** 1864 and 1865, In the Collection of The Corcoran Gallery of Art, Gift of William Wilson Corcoran, 1869

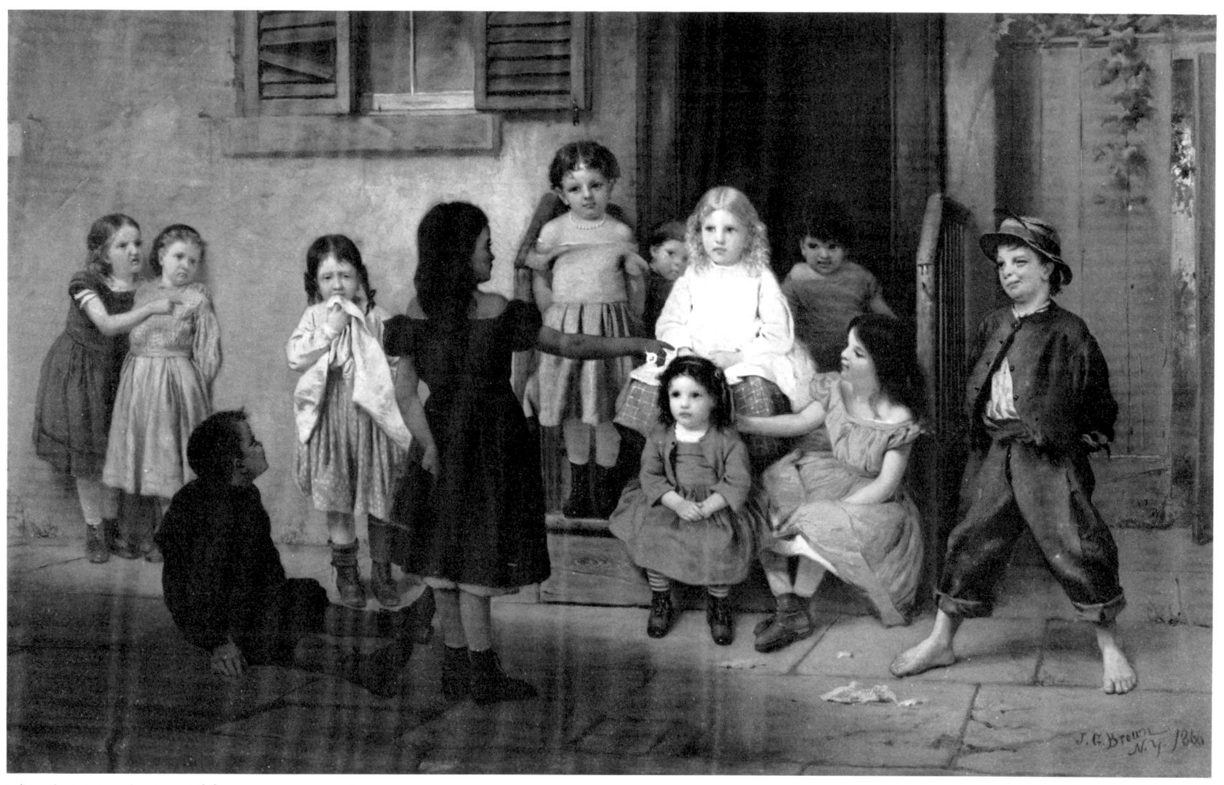

14. **The Teacher,** 1866, Anonymous Loan

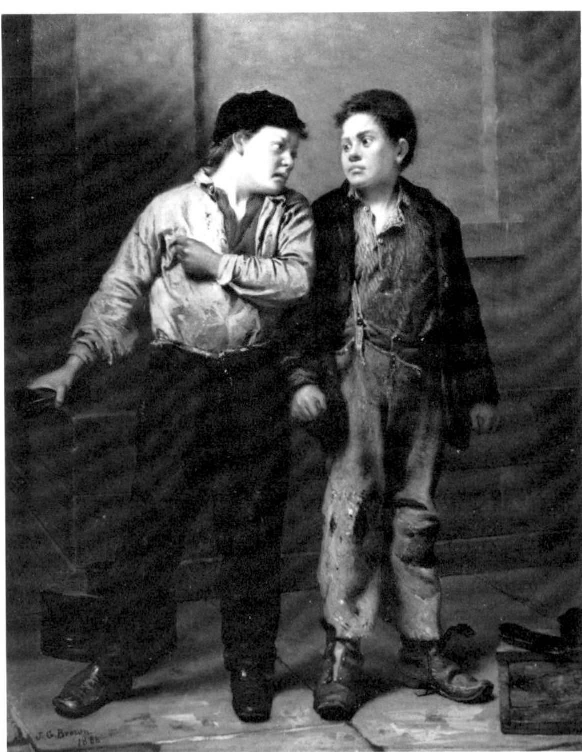

15. **When Greek Meets Greek, Then Comes the Tug of War,** 1866, Mr. and Mrs. Charles B. Tyler

him some notoriety and probably more patrons for his city subjects since he executed several spin-off smoking subjects just after this (see *Allegro* and *Penseroso,* fig. 13), as well as several group scenes involving confrontation on the city sidewalks. In *The Bully of the Neighborhood* of 1866 (Thyssen-Bornemisza Collection), a cocky, cigar-smoking boy has just broken another child's pitcher of milk, and in *The Teacher,* painted the same year (fig. 14), a young girl probably mediates between two quarreling boys. In both paintings, the children resolve their problems on their own, without adult intervention.

Elements of Brown's early city scenes became standard in his later views of city children: the pronounced narrative, which invites the viewer to imagine the story before, and especially after, the immediate episode; the charting of individual reactions of a group of children to a single event; and the sidewalk setting. Brown also picked out several features which set the location of his figures in poor city neighborhoods. In addition to the foreground sidewalk stage, he typically used a background of simplified, rundown buildings. In its most pared-down form, Brown's primary iconography of the city included a plain stone wall (or its variant of wooden doorway) and sidewalk pavement. In *The Teacher* he introduced sidewalk trash as another important symbol of city settings. Some paper litter is strewn near the feet of the mischievous boy. Though a small detail in this painting, it is significantly placed in the full light and unobstructed. Particularly for his large group scenes of the 1880's Brown exploited this motif of paper trash on the city sidewalks. To these features he added others in the 1870's, including worn posters and handbills affixed to the background wall, already a well-established iconographic motif in city scenes by other artists, and wooden packing boxes or crates for his child merchants to sit on, a device used by others but one he particularly appropriated and developed.

Most likely Brown first took up the subject that would make him famous, the city shoeshine boy, in a work dated 1866. *When Greek Meets Greek, Then Comes the Tug of War* humorously presents a confrontation between two stubborn, feisty bootblacks arguing over territory (fig. 15). Fists clenched and faces contorted, the boys stand shoulder against shoulder on a narrow stage of pavement. On the sidewalk rests the bootblack's box, the identifying feature of his trade Brown would almost always include in these paintings. At this point in his career Brown probably saw the bootblack as just another city street type, along with the newsboy and the crossing sweeper. It was only in the mid-70's that he singled out the bootblack as his special subject.

Painted prototypes for all of Brown's other images, including both country and city street types, existed in European and American art, but his interpretation of the bootblack was his own invention. Unlike newsboys and crossing sweepers, shoeshine boys rarely appeared in English or American painting before Brown. The profession itself was of recent origin in England, dating from about 1851, when young boys were recruited to shine the shoes of visitors to the Great Exhibition in London.[43] The few early English paintings of bootblack subjects date to around 1860. The most important, and perhaps the only, painted American precursor was George H. Yewell's *The Bootblack* of 1852 (New-York Historical Society). In contrast to Yewell's sober and unsentimental youth, Brown caricatured boyish bravado, remaining closer, once again, to popular illustrations of the bootblack printed in *Punch* magazine.

About 1873 Brown painted a record number of "street Arabs," the contemporary term for poor, ragged children who worked or played in

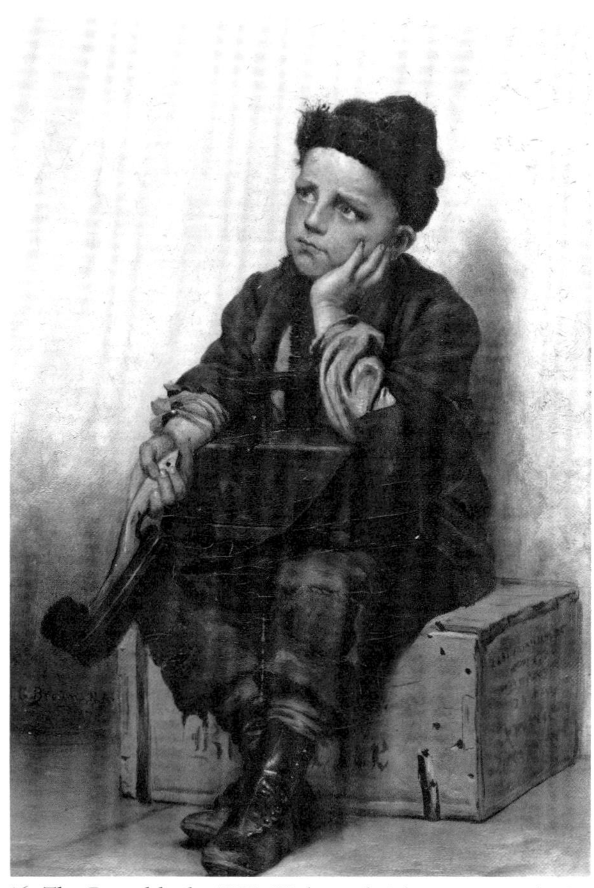

16. **The Boot-black,** 1878, Wadsworth Atheneum, Hartford, CT. Bequest of Ambrose Spencer

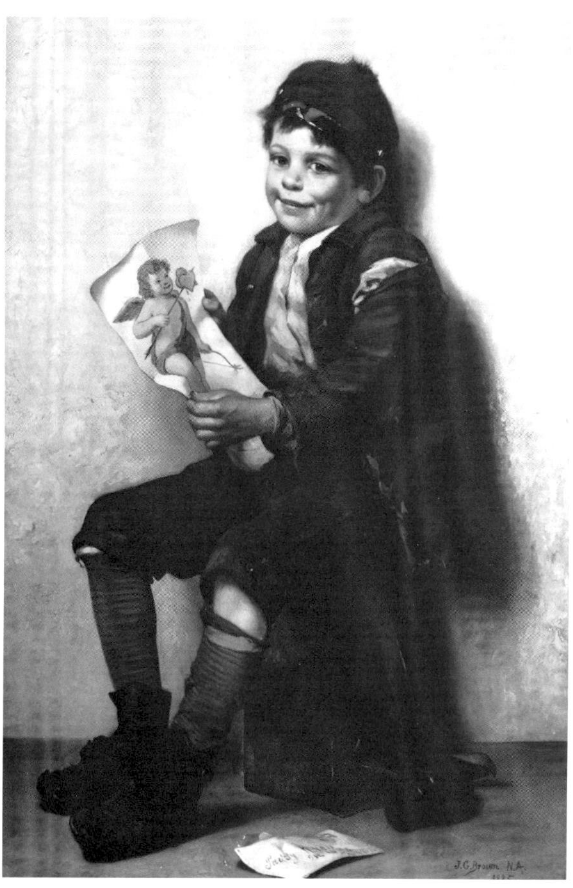

17. **Paddy's Valentine,** 1885, Mr. and Mrs. Norman Schnee

the city streets. Some eight works covered a variety of street child types, including musicians, newsboys, flower vendors, and crossing sweepers. In most of these 1873 paintings Brown portrayed street musicians, a new subject for him and one directly related to a contemporary social problem. The majority of child street musicians were young Italians, who played harp and violin on the sidewalks, even in winter weather. Many of these children belonged to an adult-run padrone system which brought young Italian children to American cities and forced them to work in the streets. The exploitation and abuse of these children was a prominent topic in the early 1870's, stimulating a rise in images, both in magazine illustration and painting, of street musicians. The subject appeared in literature too. Horatio Alger's novel *Phil the Fiddler,* written in 1872 to expose the padrone system,[44] may have directly inspired Brown's painted representations. Brown painted more street musicians over the next five years, frequently depicting Italian children, both boys and girls, playing harp and violin.

Bootblack Years

After 1875 Brown narrowed his focus on the bootblack. That year he exhibited *This Corner Don't Pay* (now lost), which represented a demoralized bootblack in deep study over his lack of business.[45] The single bootblack, especially one seated on a box (either blacking box or packing crate), became the staple of Brown's production in the 1880's and 1890's, and even into the 20th century. He also portrayed many standing bootblacks, but the seated figure remained the most frequent type, the bread and butter of his trade. *The Boot-black* of 1878 (fig. 16) and *Paddy's Valentine* of 1885 (fig. 17) are two outstanding examples of a type produced in such numbers by about 1890 that Brown was indelibly linked to it in the minds of critics and public, then and today.

In January of 1875 he was working on *Pitching Pennies* (unlocated), which presented a group of seven bootblacks before a tenement house door. *Pitching Pennies* inaugurated a string of group scenes, the most well-known being *The Passing Show* of 1877 (fig. 32). In this work five boys line up along the sidewalk, their smiling faces gazing directly out at the viewer, to watch a passing circus parade. Because the parade exists outside the painting, in Brown's typically punning humor the viewer becomes part of the scene or one of "the passing show." The boys are not identified as bootblacks or newsboys; they are typical working-class children at play on the streets. The very favorable critical response to *The Passing Show,* both at home and abroad—in Paris when it appeared at the 1878 Universal Exposition and again in London when it was shown at the Royal Academy in 1880—led to a number of similarly composed groups over the next two decades. *Dress Parade* of 1878 (private collection), *The Lost Child* of 1881 (fig. 31), and *A Jolly Lot* of 1885 (see fig. 29) picture some of the best known line-ups of fresh-faced city boys. Brown introduced compositional variations, such as a semi-circular grouping around a central character as in *The Lost Child,* but the basic formula remained a frontal view of a group of boys, usually bootblacks, shown reacting to something either outside (in front of) the painting or in the foreground of the painting.

Economic, social, and artistic factors lay behind Brown's shift in focus from middle-class country life to poor city children. While before the Civil War Americans had been aware of the rapid growth of cities and the dangers posed by deteriorating slums, from the 1870's on their awareness accelerated to near hysteria, fueled by economic instability. Four years of severe depression followed the Panic of 1873, giving rise to the first of many labor strikes. Renewed reform efforts culminated in the Progressive Era of the 1890's and early 20th century. Through all the reform movements, both before and after the Civil War, ran a common thread: the threat to society posed by children on the streets. For the middle-class, the presence of poor children living and working in—or just occupying—the streets of the slums increasingly symbolized the decay of the social fabric.[46]

The numbers of street children had already dramatically increased by the 1850's, when successive waves of immigrants, beginning in the late 1840's, caused rapid population growth in cities. Between 1850 and 1860, for example, New York City's population increased by 300,000.[47] These immigrants lived in inadequate, grossly overcrowded tenements in lower Manhattan. Their children had nowhere to be but the streets. So many families depended on the children's income from selling or scavenging that the streets teemed with roving child workers. Furthermore, jobs filled by children in an earlier time, such as apprenticeships in trades and domestic service positions, now went to adults, so more children were reduced to street work.[48] The increase in paintings of child street workers in the late 1840's and 1850's partly reflected this situation.

The crisis led to the founding of the Children's Aid Society in 1853 by Charles Loring Brace, one of the most influential figures of his time. Although Brown did not make the street urchin central to his work until the mid 1870's, his interpretation of the subject was shaped by the attitudes of a previous generation and particularly reflected the ideas of Charles Loring Brace. Brace admired the independent, hardy nature of young street boys, who had learned the hard way how to take care of themselves.[49] Of particular concern to him, and to other reformers, were the numbers of homeless or vagabond children who slept in boxes, on steam gratings, or in doorways, and survived, many just barely, through street work or theft. To preserve their spirit of independence and keep them from sinking into crime and vice, he placed thousands of city boys in foster homes in the country, and he established lodging houses in the worst slum districts of the city. The first of these houses, the Newsboys' Lodging House at Nassau and Fulton Streets, opened in 1854, and was known well enough for Brown to have been aware of it as early as the mid 1860's. He also could have known of Brace, who presented his views in articles, annual reports, and lectures through the 1850 's and 1860's and published in 1872 his full account of the Children's Aid Society, *The Dangerous Classes of New York and Twenty Years' Work Among Them.* Certainly Brown's street children conform in many ways to the ideal type as described by Brace. They embody the plucky, individual spirit Brace saw, and reveal a reverence for the joys of uninhibited boyhood. Late in life Brown claimed a special affection for his subjects. "I do not paint poor boys solely because the public likes such pictures and pays me for them," he said, "but because I love the boys myself, for I, too, was once a poor lad like them."[50]

The Boot-black, The Lost Child, Buy a Posy, A Tough Story, and *Paddy's Valentine* are typical paintings of street children ranging in date from 1878 to 1886 (figs. 16,31,18,19,17). Though their

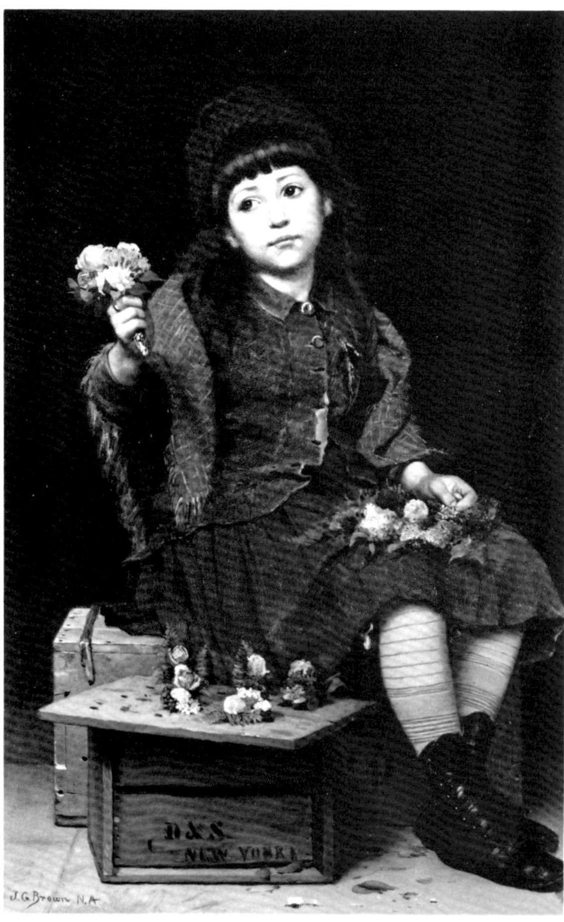

18. **Buy a Posy,** c. 1881, North Carolina Museum of Art, Raleigh, Given in memory of Mr. and Mrs. E.J. Ellisberg by their children

style is marked by greater monumentality after about 1880, with heftier children who fill the picture space more fully, Brown's interpretation remained the same. He limited the signs of poverty, conveying class and street Arab status largely through his subjects' torn and tattered clothes. Old, worn boots; drab, brown jackets and trousers; and cloth caps became part of his iconography of the city. All Brown's viewers would have identified his subjects' class immediately from the condition of their clothes. Rarely, however, did Brown paint his children in the outlandish combinations and oversized clothing that contemporary observers never failed to note. Also contrary to many 19th century accounts of street life, Brown's children are scruffy but not filthy. Their hands and bare feet are sometimes dirty, but they still have clean faces. They are healthy-looking, with fleshy limbs and full, round faces. They often smile engagingly at the viewer (fig. 46). Some contemporary reviewers seized upon these discrepancies almost immediately and criticized Brown for idealizing his subjects. Yet, at the same time, most artists and patrons would also have viewed realistic portrayals of the urban poor as an unacceptable subject for high art.

Though it is difficult to pin down who exactly bought Brown's bootblack paintings, many of his patrons were middle-class businessmen who believed, like the majority of their contemporaries, that the poor were poor because of personal failings, not because of economic forces beyond their control. This gospel of self-help shaped most attempts at social reform and partially explains why Brown did not paint realistic images of oppression. His patrons wanted images which conformed to middle-class ideals of entrepreneurship and industry. Whether or not they themselves had risen from humble beginnings, and some of them certainly had, they probably subscribed to the popular view that street work was preparation for business life rather than child labor.[51] Brown himself voiced these ideas late in his life, when he claimed repeatedly that many of his models had gone on to become successful businessmen.

Brown was not painting the lowest level of street existence, the child beggars and thieves, the rough street gangs, or the prostitutes; he was presenting working-class poor. Through certain conventions he created the image of independent, streetwise children who made their own way. Furthermore, while many viewers—and critics—would have perceived Brown's boys as homeless, many children on the streets actually belonged to families whom they helped support. Many others were not technically orphans but left voluntarily, preferring the streets to an abusive or intolerable home.[52] Whether Brown intended his children to be homeless, they do not look uncared-for. This is particularly true of his young girls, who in reality were less apt to be homeless than boys. The young girl in *Buy a Posy,* for example (fig. 18), wears worn but decent clothes, clean stockings, neat shoes, and above all, a hand-knitted hat, all signs of home care. Brown himself remarked that often the real street Arabs he recruited on the streets to model for him would show up at his studio all cleaned and scrubbed,[53] presumably by their mothers.

In his group scenes, such as *The Lost Child* and *A Tough Story,* Brown transmitted other values besides hard work and independence. He created an ideal of community, of belonging to a social group, within the urban milieu many middle-class observers perceived as impersonal.

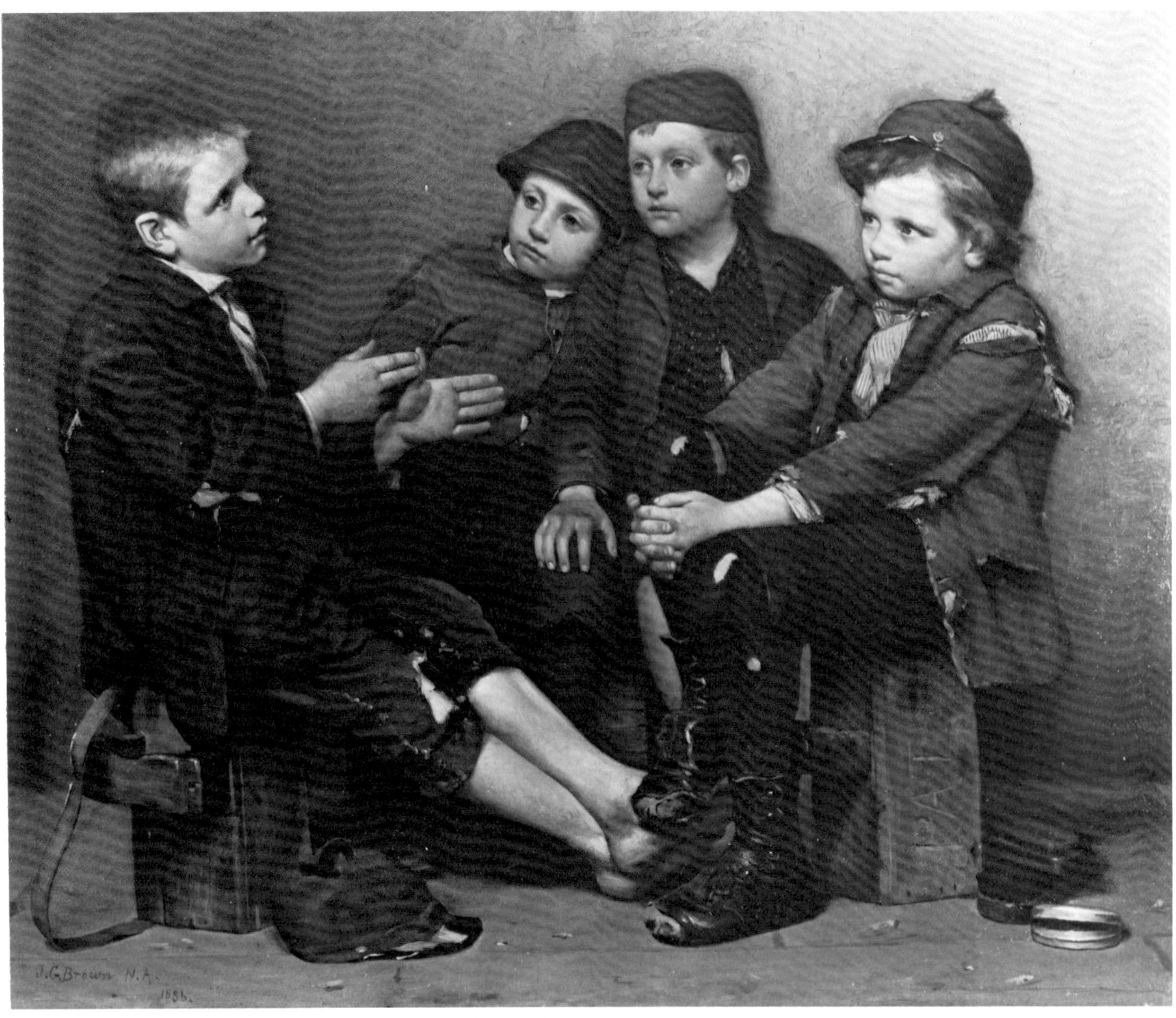

19. **A Tough Story,** 1886, North Carolina Museum of Art, Raleigh

In *The Lost Child* (fig. 31) boys of all ages rally to aid a small girl. Although one of the youths is a delivery boy, the rest are not identified as having any occupation. While street children represent freedom from society's rules, they are not without a moral sense or a code of chivalry. They stick together and help each other, bound by a common plight and sometimes a common trade. In *A Tough Story,* for example (fig. 19), young bootblacks listen sympathetically to a colleague. As early as *The Beggars* of 1863 (fig. 12) Brown made this spirit of camraderie his principal theme. In his paintings street life offered a sense of community, and it is quite possible that he was portraying the truth. In any case, Brown needed to manufacture this communal life even if it did not exist, because it reassured his patrons and because it was a personal ideal he consistently expressed in the rest of his paintings.

Brown's community of street boys is multi-ethnic as well. He very obviously depicted boys of several nationalities in his paintings and often included one black child in the groups. A reviewer described the boys in *The Lost Child* as belonging to the "German, Irish, Irish-American, English, or Jewish types of character."[54] The red-headed boy is clearly Irish, and further to the right some of the boys are most likely German. In *A Tough Story,* the boy at the far right is identified as Irish; the name "Pat" is scratched into his boot-black box. Before the 1880's the majority of immigrants were Irish and German, a distribution reflected in Brown's paintings. Some of the boys Brown painted were probably also poor, native-born Americans, who came from the farms to the city in great numbers by the 1870's. Brown's inclusion of different nationalities was not total idealization. While he probably exaggerated the ethnic diversity of his groups, it is true that street gangs were largely made up of all the nationalities on the block.[55] A street child's trade, or occupation, could also cut across ethnic boundaries, uniting all bootblacks, for instance.

Brown's paintings and Charles Loring Brace's writings express ideals also found in Horatio Alger's novels. In fact, Alger was influenced by Brace's ideas and became a frequent visitor to the Newsboys' Lodging House.[56] Alger moved to New York in the spring of 1866 and wrote his first and most famous novel, *Ragged Dick,* that fall. In this, as in other books, he gave high praise to Brace's efforts to save street children. He cast the hero of *Ragged Dick* as a bootblack, and based the story and characters on real street children he encountered. Brown's earliest bootblack (fig. 15), painted just before the appearance of Alger's novel, could have been an illustration for feisty, cheeky, independent Ragged Dick, so close was his characterization to Alger's. The popular success of *Ragged Dick,* which inspired a series of five more novels within the next three years, could not have escaped Brown. The books popularized the notion of the naturally noble, hard-working, bold, and courageous street boy who earns his way to respectability,[57] and no doubt they helped to create a market for Brown's paintings. There are important differences between Brown's painted bootblacks and Alger's literary ones, however. Ragged Dick is presented as atypical of the mass of street children. Bonafide orphans, Dick and his friend Fosdick are naturally good, honest, and industrious, but most other bootblacks in the book are lazy or mean.

Brace's ideas also shaped the thinking of newspaper reporter Jacob Riis, whose exposés of urban decay began appearing in the mid-1880's. When Riis documented his 1890 book, *How the Other Half Lives,* with his own highly realistic photographs of urban slums and poor street children, he inaugurated an era of photojournalism in the service of social reform.[58] By the 1890's Brown must have been aware of the gritty realism of Riis' photographs. In spite of this new and powerful example, Brown's paintings remained relatively the same.

English social realist art of the 1870's may be a possible artistic source for Brown's emphasis on urban poor, but not for his interpretation or style. Artists like Luke Fildes, Hubert von Herkomer, and Frank Holl painted biting, unsentimental, emotionally powerful indictments of an oppressive social system, though they did not focus particularly on street children. Brown could have known works by these English artists through reproduction as early as 1870.[59]

Few American artists painted urban child workers immediately following the Civil War. The artist to most often include urban poverty among his subjects in the late 1860's and early 1870's was probably the little-known Constant Mayer, who was born and trained in France. His 1869 painting of two young girls in a tenement interior, for instance, was described in the contemporary press, along with one called, suggestively, *Give Us This Day Our Daily Bread.*[60] The widely read magazine, *Harper's Weekly,* printed illustrations of poor street children in the late 1860's, but devoted more space to poor and working-class life in the next decade. Painted newsboys, vendors, and musicians also grew in number through the 1870's and 1880's. Few artists besides J.G. Brown attempted to paint bootblacks, however, most likely because he was so identified with that subject by 1880. Probably inspired by Brown, Thomas Waterman Wood painted several street types in 1879, including a young bootblack reading the news and a newsboy counting his cash (unlocated). Two of Brown's pupils, Gilbert Gaul and Ferdinand Schuchardt, also painted urban poverty themes either during or just after their study with Brown in the late 1870's and early 1880's. Brown had followers as well, notably Karl Witkowski, who imitated his urchins so skillfully in the 1890's that his paintings are often confused with Brown's today. Despite these other artists, Brown remained the major painter of urban poor children.

The 1880's can be considered Brown's bootblack decade. In that period he painted most of his best single-figure and group scenes, they were reproduced and shown most widely, and they pushed other subject matter to the background. He concentrated on the single bootblack placed in various limited settings. As before, no adults appear in the paintings, and aside from works like *Jersey Mud* (fig. 20), rarely are the boys shown actually shining shoes. In the earliest paintings, those from about 1875 to 1885, he seems to have favored a light (cream) stucco wall, roughly painted, as a background. Around 1888 he often placed his figures against a dark green, panelled wooden door or white

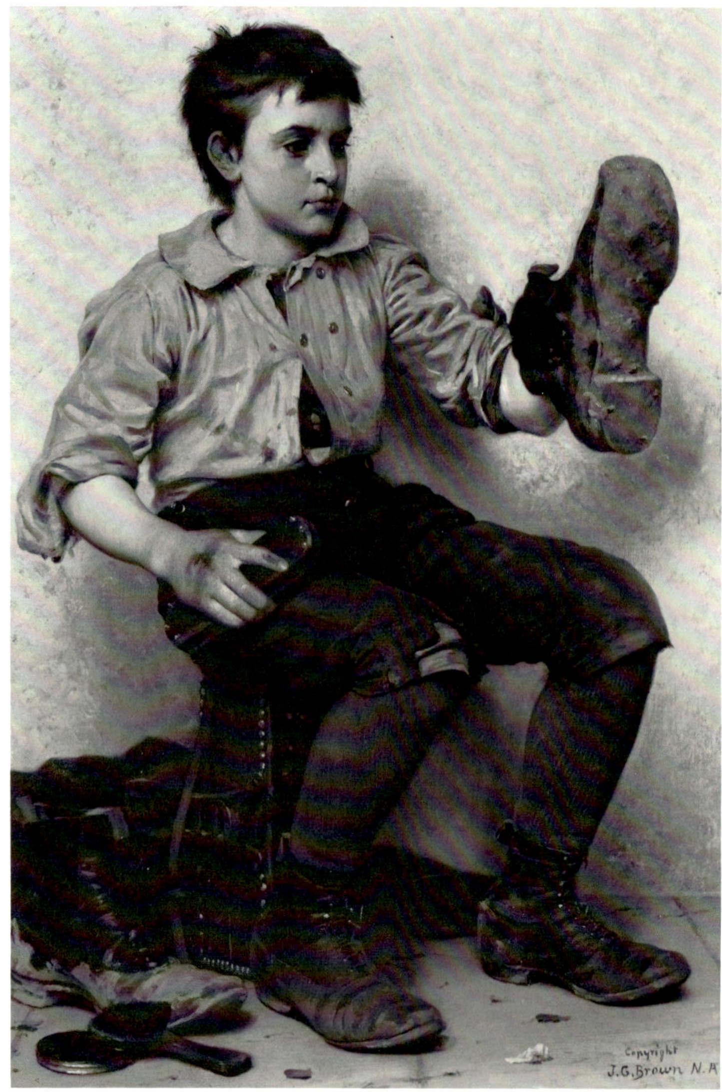

20. **Jersey Mud,** c. 1885-1890, Lent by the High Museum of Art, Atlanta, Georgia; gift of Mr. and Mrs. George E. Missbach

wooden door with worn, peeling surface. About 1880 he introduced one of his most popular compositional variations, the bootblack and his dog. Most often the dog stands on the boy's lap or on a wooden box filled with straw while the boy teaches the dog tricks or receives sympathy from his pet. By the end of the century Brown was producing these in endless numbers and greatly declining quality.

Although Brown continued to paint bootblacks in the 1890's, his compositions became repetitious, his poses less natural, and his technique dry and perfunctory. The change is most marked in his group scenes, which by the mid 1890's had become static arrangements of many figures in expanded settings. In some ways this development in Brown's art reflects actual changes in the bootblack profession. After 1890 young shoeshine boys were gradually replaced by adults who operated fixed shoeshine stands.[61] Just before his death Brown lamented the disappearance of the old-time bootblack, claiming that modern commercialism had driven these "picturesque" characters from the street. Greatly romanticizing their existence, he asserted that street life had made them "alert, strong, healthy little chaps, with elastic bodies and frank, courageous faces."[62] By 1900 Brown was painting past history.

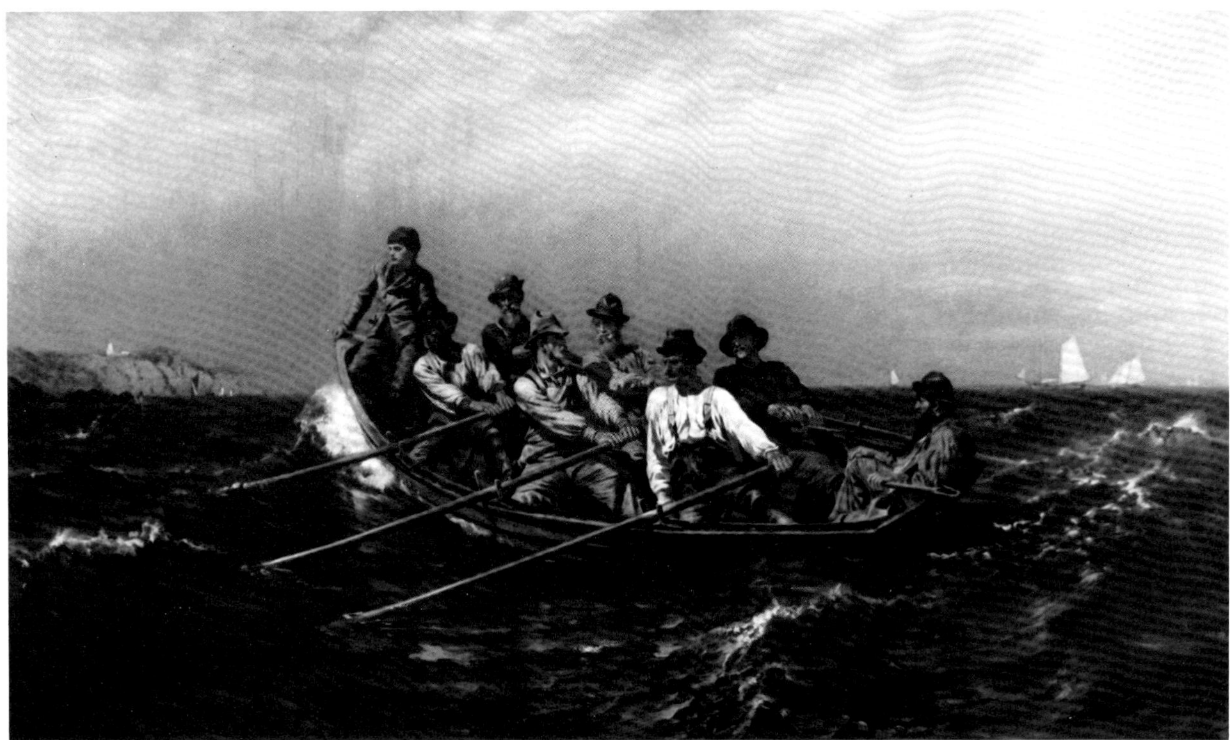

21. **Pulling for Shore,** 1878, The Chrysler Museum, Norfolk, Virginia, Gift of Walter P. Chrysler, Jr.

New Subjects

From the late 1870's on, while he was turning out the bootblacks, Brown was also investigating a new subject matter: adult men, either singly or in groups. The best known adult subject is his masterpiece, *The Longshoremen's Noon,* painted in 1879 (fig. 30). In this large-scale, complex scene of dockworkers at lunch-time Brown raised genre painting to the level of history painting. Unlike previous works on the theme of laborers by English artists Ford Maddox Brown and William Bell Scott, Brown painted a group of laborers at rest, conversing harmoniously, rather than heroically working. The men represent a range of nationalities, including German and Irish among others, all gathered together in peaceful exchange. The reality of labor unrest and violent strike such as had occurred in 1877 seems especially remote. As in his groups of street children, Brown promoted an ideal of community.

His interest in the subject of working men dates from his experience at Grand Menan Island, where he spent the summers of 1877 and 1878 painting the hardy fishermen. Numerous freely brushed oil studies and paintings resulted from these trips (figs. 41 and 53), as well as one large, ambitious group scene of fishermen in a boat, *Pulling for Shore,* of 1878 (fig. 21). Brown's attitude was mainly objective in these works; he recorded the prosaic activities of catching, cleaning, and weighing fish and did not dwell on the threat of elemental nature or the hardship of existence. Instead, he was most interested in the men's rugged faces and, once again, in the larger idea of communal life.

Brown painted men in groups for only a few years; then in the 1880's he found another adult subject in old men and women in rural interiors. These paintings grew increasingly important in the 1890's as his bootblacks approached mass production. His nostalgic scenes of old people evoke an uncomplicated, rural past and represent the survival of the shrewd Yankee spirit in the country. In turning to this subject Brown followed the lead of other American artists, notably Eastman Johnson, who painted salty old men in rustic interiors as early as the mid 1870's. Thomas Hovenden, Enoch Wood Perry, and Thomas Waterman Wood all painted old people in the 1880's.

Probably Brown's interest was sparked by a visit in 1881 to Ellenville, New York, where Edward Lamson Henry worked. Henry's paintings of local Cragsmoor characters may have inspired Brown to execute several interior

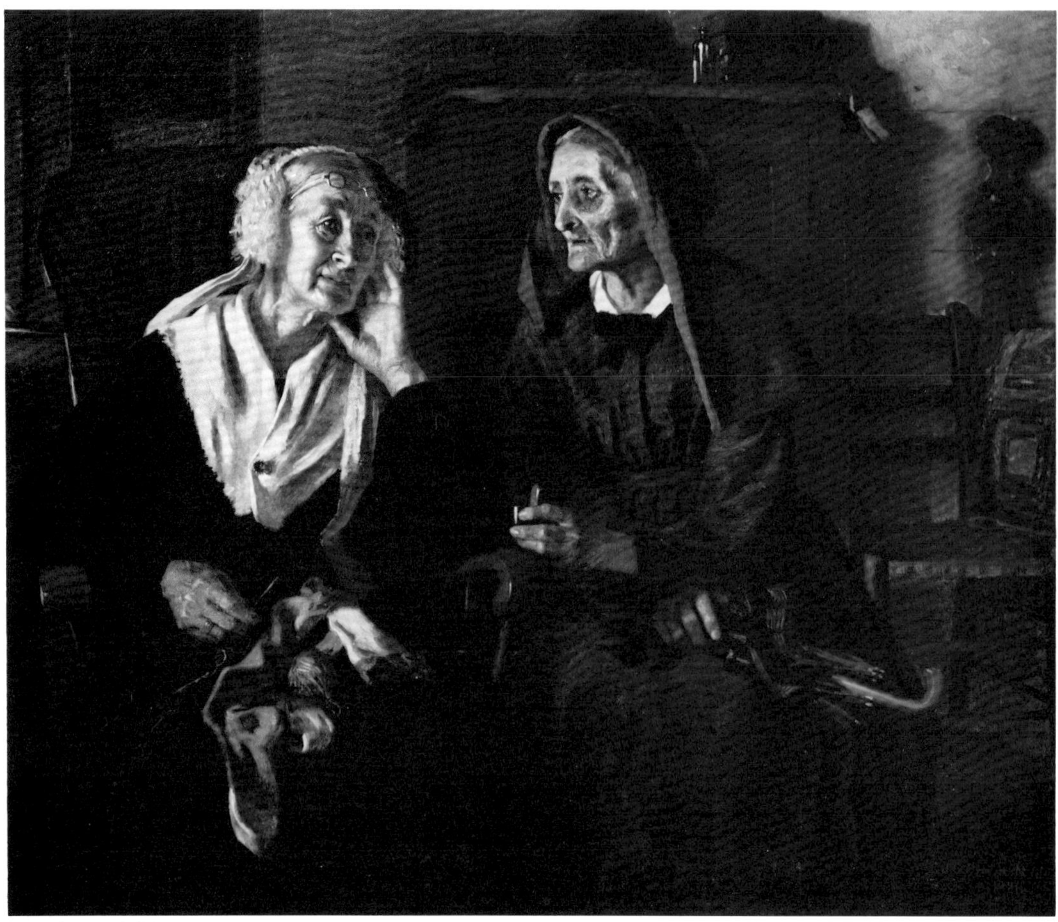

22. **The Neighbors,** 1881, Lent by the High Museum of Art, Atlanta, Georgia; gift of Mr. and Mrs. George E. Missbach

scenes like *The Neighbors,* dated 1881 (fig. 22), which depicts two old women conversing in a dimly lit room. A painting from about 1893 called *Home Comforts* (fig. 23) continues the theme of old folks but shows the stiffening of brushwork and wealth of detail common in later works of this type. By the 1900's Brown was spending his summers in Vermont, which provided the setting and models for many of his rustic interiors. The woman in *Home Comforts* is even more obviously a relic of bygone days, surrounded by symbols of age and country life. Typically Brown's subjects read Bibles or meditate over past memories amidst a profusion of accessories that contrasts greatly with the spare settings of his bootblack paintings. For old men Brown developed a favorite composition involving one or more stock characters, shrewd, bewhiskered old farmers, cogitating in barn interiors. *To Decide the Question,* for instance, of about 1897 (Metropolitan Museum of Art) presents three farmers ostensibly discussing the merits of a horse. In paintings like these he portrayed the survival of the Yankee spirit, but in other works he captured the pathetic loneliness of old age.

* * * * * * *

Brown's real genius lay in his ability to tell a story and to sense the direction of popular taste. His genre scenes blended English Victorian and American anecdotal traditions in a style of descriptive realism that varied little throughout his career. His style and subjects remained in tune with public taste. At the height of his critical success in the mid-70's, he began developing city street scenes as an alternate subject matter to idyllic country views; when artists and patrons moved away from country subjects in the 1880's, Brown was ready. At the height of his production of urban scenes, he began developing another alternate subject, this time old folks in the country. He was gifted, remarked one observer, with a business sense.[63]

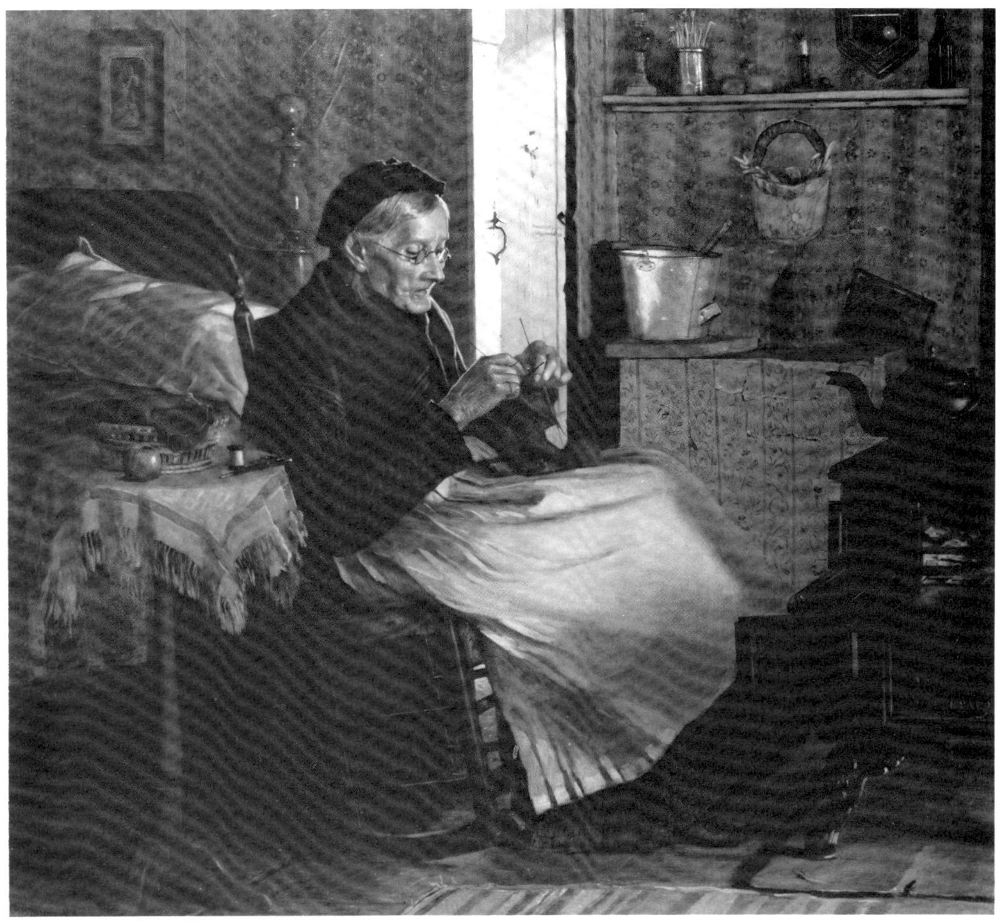

23. **Home Comforts,** c. 1893, Charles and Ann Spaulding

His popularity was legend even in his own time. Critics helped create this legend by repeatedly claiming that Brown's paintings sold immediately and for high prices, a feat they considered remarkable because so many American patrons preferred European paintings at this time. According to *Harper's Weekly* as early as 1880, for example, Brown always had enough buyers "to keep his studio well emptied of pictures. Today it contains not a single finished canvas. Hard times, dull times, bad times, he knows nothing of except by heresay."[64] He did not, however, sell all his paintings at once, nor did he always get the price he asked. While he commanded steadily rising prices (his major works selling for as much as $2500), the price of an average painting was not particularly high; he managed well because he sold in quantity.

Like a number of post-Civil War genre painters, however, Brown's reputation declined rapidly after his death, obscuring his modest but solid achievement. Showing remarkable solidarity of opinion, early 20th century critics and historians uniformly dismissed him for compromising his art in order to make money. Many 19th century critics in fact objected to Brown's idealized street children and particularly denigrated his popular support. The *New York Times* reviewer, for example, rarely sympathetic to Brown, noted in 1880 that his view of three urchin boys was drawing greater crowds than any other painting on exhibit and complained that, "Artists will not find much art in it, but the public finds plenty of food for merriment."[65] Other critics similarly charged that Brown's easy humor and undemanding sentiment, along with the polished realism of his painting style, made him a hit with an unsophisticated public. Yet prominent collectors of the period bought Brown's paintings in addition to affluent businessmen and probably more ordinary middle-class people. Beyond that, middle-class urban and rural households must have displayed the prints and photographs reproducing his paintings. "Everywhere throughout the land, if not throughout the world, in the houses of the highest as well as the lowest, are to be found the originals or copies of Mr. Brown's bootblacks,'' claimed a writer in 1899.[66]

It is easy to point out that in his idealized scenes of urban poverty Brown was no social realist, yet he focused public attention on working-class, immigrant children and established them as fit subjects for art. He contributed greatly to the iconography of city life and served as an important forerunner to the artists of the Ash Can School, who painted the vitality of urban, lower-class life at the turn of the century. As a result of his immense popularity in his time, Brown has always been associated with one image, the city shoeshine boy. Acknowledging this a few months before his death, he remarked, ''When J.G. Brown is no more, those who come after me will be rummaging about this studio and they will discover scores of canvases which will show, I hope, that I was not a painter of one idea.''[67] While he painted landscapes, portraits, outdoor rural scenes, and old people in abundance, ultimately his most original contribution lay with that ''one idea.''

1. *Harper's Weekly,* Vol. XXVI, April 15, 1882, p. 231.
2. Charles de Kay, ''Veteran of Academicians is J.G. Brown,'' *The New York Times,* November 13, 1904, pt. 4, p. 1.
3. Ishmael, ''Through the New York Studios,'' *The Illustrated American,* Vol. 6, no. 65, May 16, 1891, p. 621.
4. George Sheldon, *Hours with Art and Artists,* New York, 1882, p. 152.
5. George Sheldon, *American Painters,* New York, 1879, p. 141.
6. ''Mr. John G. Brown, Artist, Dies of Pneumonia at 81,'' *The New York Herald,* February 9, 1913, p. 8.
7. Lindsay Errington, *Master Class, Robert Scott Lauder and his Pupils,* Edinburgh, National Galleries of Scotland, 1983, p. 64.
8. ''The Crossing-Sweeper,'' *The Aldine Press,* Vol. VIII, no. 10, 1877, p. 328.
9. Ishmael, ''Through the New York Studios,'' 1891, p. 621.
10. A letter dated 1909 from Brown to the Metropolitan Museum of Art, New York, American Painting department files, supplies specific dates for some key events.
11. Ishmael, ''Through the New York Studios,'' 1891, p. 621.
12. Clark S. Marlor, *A History of the Brooklyn Art Association with an Index of Exhibitions,* New York, 1974, p. 5.
13. ''John G. Brown,'' *Harper's Weekly,* Vol. XXIV, no. 1224, June 12, 1880, p. 374.
14. ''The Painter of Street Arabs,'' *The Art Amateur,* Vol. 31, no. 6, November 1894, p. 125.
15. See Marlor, *A History of the Brooklyn Art Association,* pp. 6-13, 23.
16. Chief among them was Seymour Guy. Like Brown, Guy was born and trained in England, emigrated in almost the same year, and painted scenes of children. Their friendship probably reinforced Brown's polished, realist style and preference for English Victorian subjects. Although Guy also painted occasional scenes of street children as early as the 1860's, he probably did not influence Brown's choice of this subject matter.
17. *Harper's Weekly,* Vol. XXIV, no. 1224, June 12, 1880, p. 374.
18. I thank Sally Mills, Assistant Curator of American Paintings at the Fine Arts Museums of San Francisco, for her discovery of an 1876 map of Fort Lee showing property owned by a J.G. Brown. I am also indebted to Merl M. Moore, Jr., for providing me with Brown's passport application, which shows that Brown became a naturalized citizen in Bergen County, New Jersey, in 1864.
19. See Kathryn M. Heleniak, *William Mulready,* New Haven and London, 1980, p. 75-121.
20. Susan P. Casteras, *Down the Garden Path: Courtship Culture and its Imagery in Victorian Painting,* Ph.D. dissertation, 4 vols., Yale University, 1977, Vol. I, pp. 205-215, 225, 259-260.
21. I wish to thank Susan Casteras, Assistant Curator of Paintings, Yale Center for British Art, for calling my attention to both Egley and *Punch* magazine.
22. William H. Gerdts, ''Through a Glass Brightly: The American Pre-Raphaelites and their Still Lifes and Nature Studies,'' in Linda S. Ferber and William H. Gerdts, *The New Path, Ruskin and the American Pre-Raphaelites,* The Brooklyn Museum, 1985, p. 40-44.
23. *Catalogue of the Private Collection of Oil Paintings, by American Artists, Made by Samuel P. Avery,* Henry H. Leeds and Miner, February 4, 1867, no. 15. The painting, originally shown in 1864 at the Brooklyn Art Association, was probably commissioned by Avery. See also Annette Blaugrund, ''The Tenth Street Studio Building: A Roster, 1857-1895,'' *The American Art Journal,* Vol. XIV, no. 2, Spring 1982, p. 64-71, for Moore's studio dates.
24. *The New Path, Ruskin and the American Pre-Raphaelites,* catalogue entry by Annette Blaugrund, p. 244.
25. They were: *Playing Mother, The Queen of the Woods [The Little Queen of the Woods], Little Bo-Peep, The Three Tomboys,* and *The Maiden's Prayer,* all published by Prang; and *Maud Muller,* published by William Schaus.
26. Like many Brown paintings, *The Music Lesson* may not bear its original title. *A Game Two Can Play At,* the title given to an undated engraving after the painting, is more characteristic of Brown. Original titles are not known for the following works discussed here: *Young Girl in a New York Garden, The Cider Mill, The Beggars, The Teacher, The Boot-black, Paddy's Valentine, Buy a Posy.* If not original titles, *View of the Palisades, Hudson River; The Berry Boy; A Tough Story;* and *Silver Birches* are probably close to the original. *Pulling for Shore* was originally titled *Pull for the Shore* when exhibited.
27. Natalie Spassky et al., *American Paintings in the Metropolitan Museum of Art,* Vol. II, New York, 1985, p. 339.
28. Brown's trip is documented by notices in the *New York Evening Post* of July 11, July 25, August 11, September 9, and Septemer 14, 1870. I am grateful to Merl M. Moore, Jr., for calling my attention to these notices.

29. *Harper's Weekly,* Vol. XXIV, no. 1224, June 12, 1880, p. 373.

30. *New York Evening Post,* May 4, 1872, p. 1, identifies the subject.

31. *New York Evening Post,* December 31, 1873, p. 2.

32. Brown had begun work on the composition by June, 1874, according to the *New York Evening Post,* June 23, 1874.

33. See James Yarnall and William H. Gerdts, *The National Museum of American Art's Index to American Art Exhibition Catalogues,* Boston, 1986, Vol. I, p. 483-489.

34. I am indebted to Sally Mills for research on this painting. A smaller version of the painting, dated 1865, was offered at Brown's studio sale. See *The Finished Pictures and Studies Left by the Late J.G. Brown, N.A.*, American Art Galleries, February 9 and 10, 1914, no. 8.

35. For a discussion of the country boy in art and literature see Sarah Burns, "Barefoot Boys and Other Country Children: Sentiment and Ideology in Nineteenth-Century American Art," *The American Art Journal,* Vol. XX, no. 1, 1988, p. 24-50.

36. Yarnall and Gerdts, *Index to American Art Exhibition Catalogues,* p. 483-489.

37. Howard Rodee, *Scenes of Rural and Urban Poverty in Victorian Painting and Their Development, 1850 to 1890,* Ph.D. dissertation, Columbia University, 1975, p. 129-132.

38. David Duff, *Punch on Children, A Panorama 1845-1865,* London, 1975; and Susan P. Casteras, " 'The Gulf of destitution on whose brink they hang'; Images of Life on the Streets in Victorian Art," in Julian Treuherz et al., *Hard Times, Social Realism in Victorian Art,* London, 1987, p. 133.

39. I thank Timothy Burgard for providing information on this painting.

40. William H. Gerdts, "Henry Inman: Genre Painter," *The American Art Journal,* Vol. IX, no. 1, May 1977, p. 41, and Patricia Hills, "Images of Rural America in the Works of Eastman Johnson, Winslow Homer, and Their Contemporaries," in *The Rural Vision, France and America in the Late Nineteenth Century,* Hollister Sturges, ed., Omaha, 1987, p. 65-67.

41. Gerdts, "Henry Inman," p. 41.

42. All accounts of Brown's life incorrectly state that *The First Cigar* was first exhibited in 1860 at the National Academy of Design. The work first appeared in December 1863 or January 1864 at a Dodworth Building studio exhibition.

43. Gabriel Weisberg, *The Realist Tradition; French Painting and Drawing 1830-1900,* Cleveland Museum of Art, 1980, catalogue entry by Kenneth McConkey, p. 195-197.

44. Gary Scharnhorst with Jack Bales, *The Lost Life of Horatio Alger, Jr.,* Bloomington, Ind., 1985, pp. 95-97, 176-177.

45. *Boston Evening Transcript,* November 24, 1875, p. 6.

46. Paul Boyer, *Urban Masses and Moral Order in America, 1820-1920,* Cambridge, Mass., 1978, see especially chp. 6. Also Christine Stansell, *City of Women, Sex and Class in New York, 1789-1860,* New York, 1986, chp. 10.

47. Stansell, *City of Women,* p. 198.

48. *Ibid.*, p. 203.

49. Charles Loring Brace, *The Dangerous Classes and Twenty Years' Work Among Them,* New York, 1872, esp. p. 97-100. Brace's discussion of street boys on these pages is particularly close to Brown's characterization. Brace noted the boys were kind to one another, "light-hearted," generous, and "always ready for the smallest joke." For a full discussion of Brace's attitudes and writings see Boyer, *Urban Masses and Moral Order,* chp. 6, and Stansell, *City of Women,* chp. 10.

50. "A Painter of Street Urchins," *The New York Times Magazine,* August 27, 1899, p. 4.

51. See Robert H. Bremner, *From the Depths, The Discovery of Poverty in the United States,* New York, 1956, and Viviana Zelizer, *Pricing the Priceless Child, The Changing Social Value of Children,* New York, 1985, p. 79-82.

52. Stansell, *City of Women,* p. 207-208, explores the "complicated geography of family life" in the slums.

53. "The Painter of Street Arabs," *The Art Amateur,* Vol. 31, no. 6, November 1894, p. 125.

54. *The Art Amateur,* Vol. V, no. 6, November 1881, p. 113.

55. David Nasaw, *Children of the City,* New York, 1985, p. 30-32, describing the later period of 1900 to 1920; the situation was most likely the same in earlier decades. I thank David Nasaw for pointing out the influx of young farm boys into the city.

56. Scharnhorst and Bales, *The Lost Life of Horatio Alger, Jr.,* p. 76-80.

57. Alger's heroes strove for respectability, not riches (*Ibid.*, p. 150).

58. Peter B. Hales, *Silver Cities, The Photography of American Urbanization, 1839-1915,* Philadelphia, 1984, p. 163-178. Echoing Brace and Brown, even Riis could write that the "Street Arab has all the faults and all the virtues of the lawless life he leads," and admire his "sturdy independence, love of freedom and absolute self-reliance." See Jacob Riis, *How the Other Half Lives,* New York, 1890, reprint Williamstown, Mass., 1972, p. 196-97.

59. Luke Fildes' *Homeless and Hungry* was reproduced in *Harper's Weekly,* Vol. XIV, no. 679, January 1, 1870, though the artist was not identified. French art of the 1880's offers intriguing parallels in subject matter. Jules Bastien-Lepage, whose paintings were known in America, painted a *London Bootblack* in 1882, and works by Fernand Pelez were also known in this country. A small sketch of Pelez's *Martyr,* showing a dead or exhausted young street merchant, appeared on the cover of *The Art Amateur,* Vol. 13, no. 2, July 1885. Brown had already established his types of street children by the late 1870's, however, probably without recourse to French art.

60. "Art Notes," *The Albion,* July 10, 1869, p. 398.

61. Nasaw, *Children of the City,* p. 187-88.

62. " 'The Street Gamin Has Vanished from New York,' " *The New York Times,* November 17, 1912, pt. 5, p. 9.

63. S. G. W. Benjamin, "A Painter of the Streets," *The Magazine of Art,* Vol. V, 1882, p. 266.

64. *Harper's Weekly,* Vol. XXIV, no. 1224, June 12, 1880, p. 374.

65. "The Artists' Fund," *The New York Times,* February 12, 1880, p. 8.

66. "A Painter of Street Urchins," *The New York Times Magazine,* August 27, 1899, p. 4.

67. "Mr. John G. Brown, Artist, Dies of Pneumonia at 81," *The New York Herald,* February 9, 1913, p. 8.

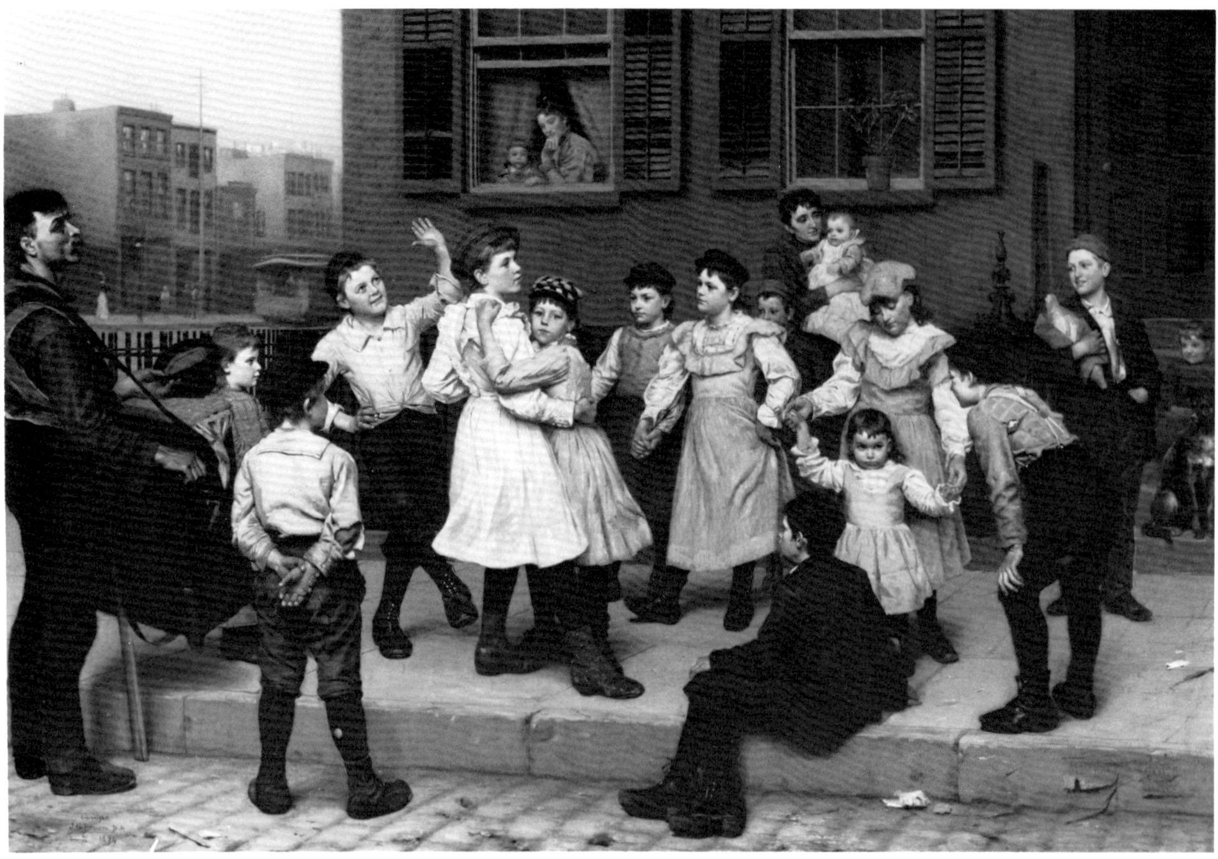

24. **The Sidewalk Dance,** 1894, Private Collection

CHRONOLOGY

1831 Born near Durham, England, on November 11.

1845 At age 14 began seven year apprenticeship as glass cutter in Newcastle.

1849-52 Studied evenings at the Newcastle School of Design with William Bell Scott.

1852-53 In Edinburgh, worked at the Holyrood Glass Factory and studied evenings at the Trustees Academy with Robert Bell Scott. Won second prize in the Antique class that spring.

1853 Spent 3 months in London in the summer.

1853 Emigrated to the United States, arriving November 11 in New York; settled in Brooklyn and found work at the Brooklyn Flint Glass Co.

1855 September 10 married Mary Owen, daughter of his employer, William Owen. Left glass factory and began career as a painter.

1856-57 Listed in Brooklyn city directory as portrait painter, with studio corner of Atlantic and Clinton Streets; lived with wife's parents at 21 Willow Place.

1856 Father-in-law died.

1857-60 Listed in Brooklyn city directory as portrait painter, living at 182 Smith Street with mother-in-law.

1857-58 Enrolled in the National Academy of Design life and antique classes taught by Thomas Seir Cummings.

1858 Exhibited at the National Academy of Design this year and every year thereafter, except 1871, until his death.

1858-59 Enrolled again at the National Academy of Design, life class only.

1859 Founding member of the Brooklyn Art Social.

1860-61 Listed Brooklyn city directory as portrait painter, home 386 Adelphi, no longer with mother-in-law. Moved studio to Tenth Street Studio Building, NYC, in summer. Kept this studio to the end of his life.

1861 Founding member Brooklyn Art Association.

1861 Daughter Charlotte born.
Elected Associate Member, National Academy of Design.

1861-62 Served on Board of Management, Brooklyn Art Association.

1863 Elected full member of National Academy of Design.

1863-69 Listed NYC directory as studio 10th St., home New Jersey.

1863 Spent August in Shelburne, N.H., hills.

1864 About this year daughter Isabelle born. Became naturalized citizen in Bergen County, N.J.

1865 Painted in Fort Lee area near or with Seymour Guy in September.

1866 Photographic reproductions of three Brown paintings published by Gellatly and Leckey, NYC.

1867 Elected member of American Society of Painters in Water Colors (later called American Watercolor Society) in March. Mary Owen Brown died in September.

1868 Chromolithograph of *Maud Muller* published by William Schaus.

1869 Chromolithograph of *Playing Mother* published by Louis Prang.
Made summer tour of New England.

1869-70 Listed NYC directory as studio 10th St.; no home listed.

1870 August and September in Europe, visited London, Scotland, and Paris. Traveled with New York art dealer John Snedecor.
Louis Prang published four more Brown paintings as chromolithographs.

1870-76 Listed NYC directory as studio 10th St., home 327 E. 30th.

1871 Married sister-in-law Emma Augusta Owen, age 18, in New York City in July.

1872 Summer in the White Mountains.
Son George Arthur born.

1873 To Catskill Mountains in July, in Catskill region in September.
Chromolithograph of *Why Don't He Come?* published by Williams and Everett.

1874 Son Oscar Irwin born.
Visited western Massachusetts and probably Ulster or Sullivan County, NY, in summer.

1875 To Pine Hill, Ulster County, NY, for summer.

1875-76 Taught portraiture as Visitor at National Academy of Design.

1876 Daughter Mabel born.

1876-77 Listed NYC directory as studio 10th St., home 250 W. 42nd. Remained at this address until 1908.

1877 Summer on Grand Menan Island, New Brunswick, painting fishermen.

1878 Son Homer Guy born.
Summer Southampton, L.I., Gloucester, Mass., and Grand Menan Island. Painted fishermen at Grand Menan.
Exhibited *The Passing Show* in France (Universal Exposition) to excellent reviews.

1879 Summer in Southampton, L.I., first, then met Gilbert Gaul in Boston as start of tour to Maine (Moosehead Lake), where camped. Also visited logging camp in Maine.

1880 *The Passing Show* exhibited in London at Royal Academy.

1881 Exhibited studies and sketches at the Brooklyn Art Association in February.
Summer at Ellenville, Ulster County, NY.

1882 Summer at Neversink, Sullivan County, NY.

1883 Daughter Florence probably born this year. Son Homer Guy died.

1886 Summer at Cragsmoor, NY, near Edward Lamson Henry.

1887-1904 Served as president of the American Watercolor Society.

1891 Summer in the Berkshire hills, western Massachusetts.

1892 Held sale of 138 paintings by auction at the Fifth Avenue Art Galleries on January 26 and 27.

1893 Served as juror for American paintings at Chicago World's Fair.

1899-1903 Served as vice-president of National Academy of Design.

1908-09 Listed NYC directory as studio 10th St., home Vermont.

1900-1913 Listed NYC directory as studio 10th St., home 346 W. 72 St. until his death.

1913 Died February 8 of pneumonia in New York City.

1914 Sale February 9 and 10 by auction of 155 paintings left in his estate.

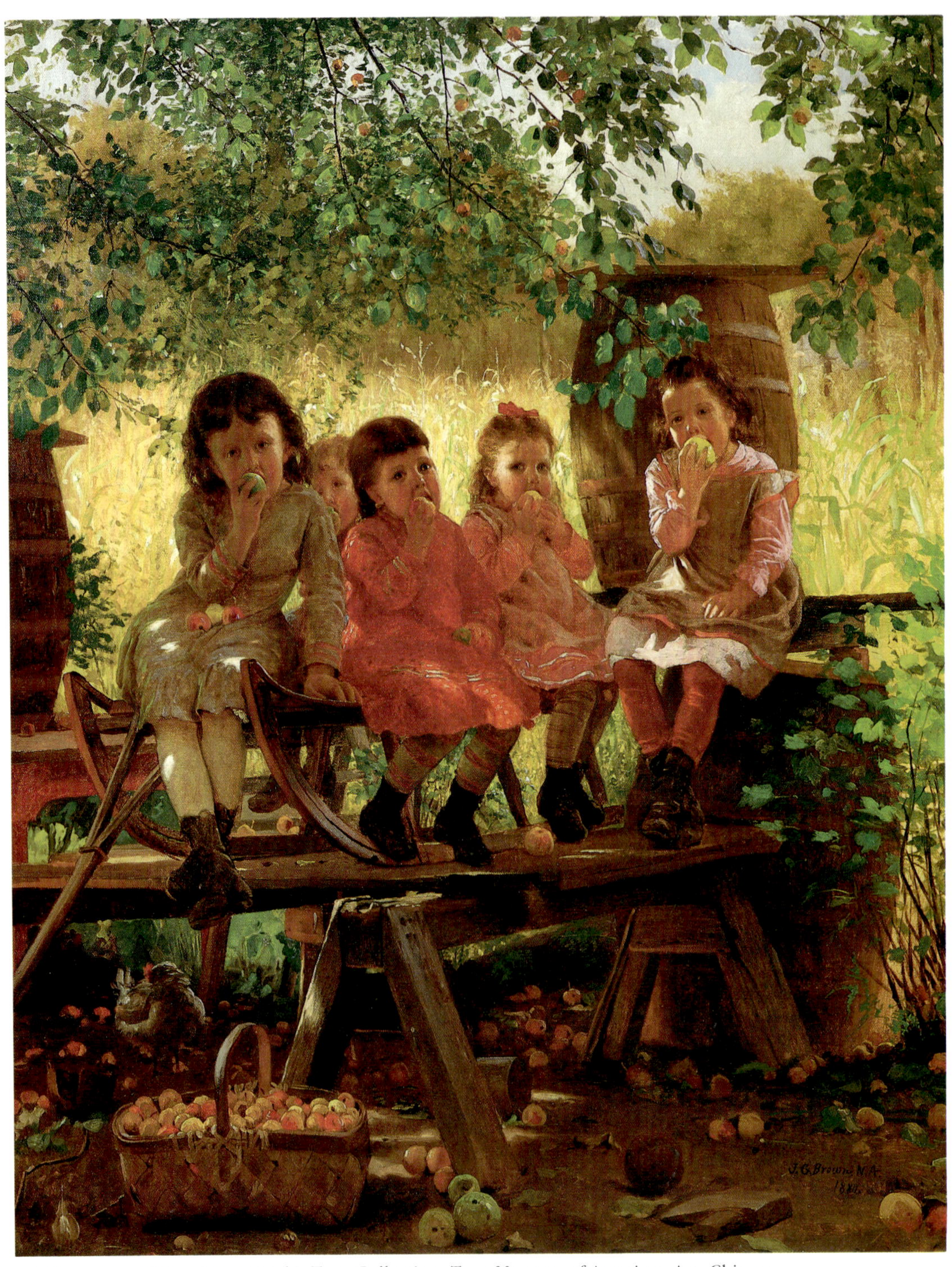

25. **The Cider Mill,** 1880, Daniel J. Terra Collection. Terra Museum of American Art, Chicago

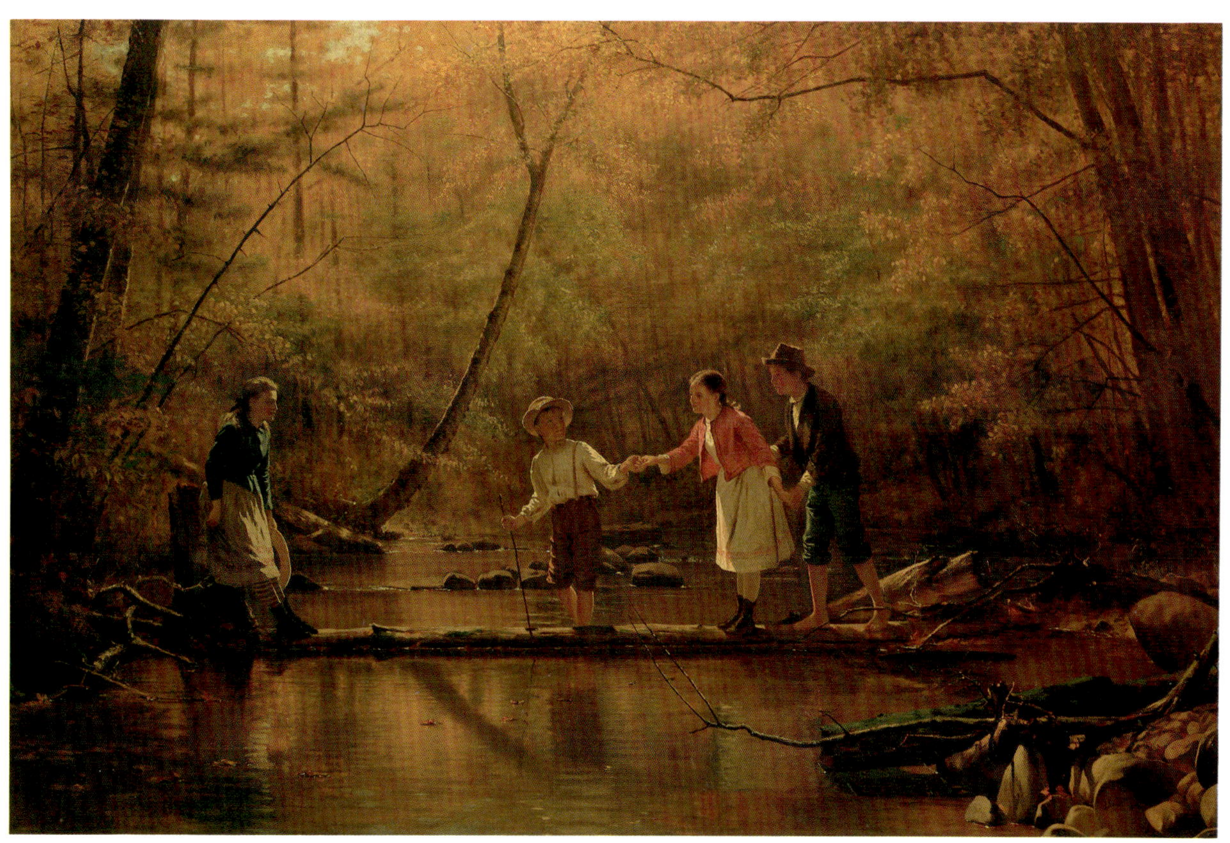

26. **The Country Gallants,** 1876, The Toledo Museum of Art; Gift of Florence Scott Libbey

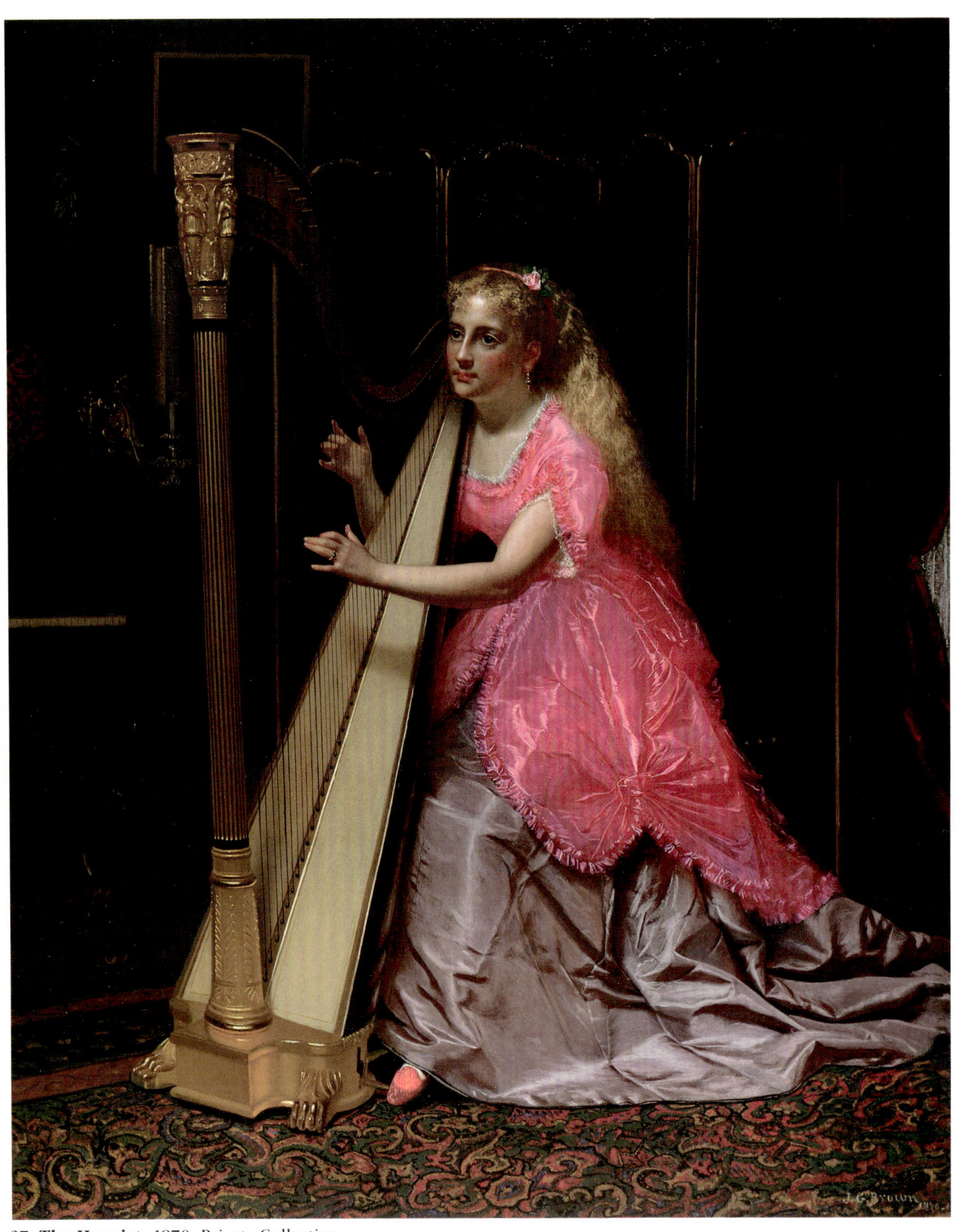

27. **The Harpist,** 1870, Private Collection

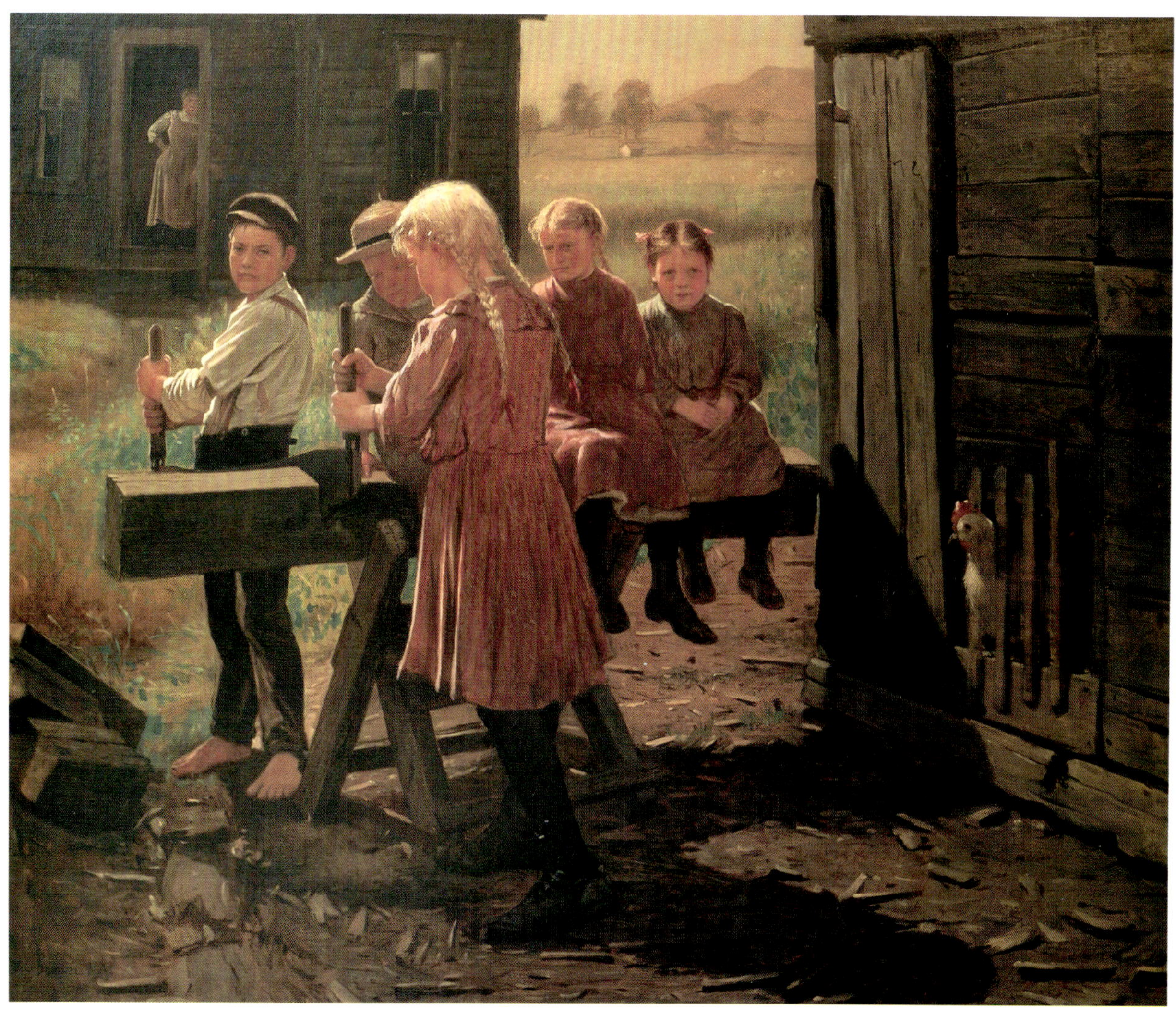

28. **The Industrious Family,** c. 1890's, Marge and Leslie Greenbaum

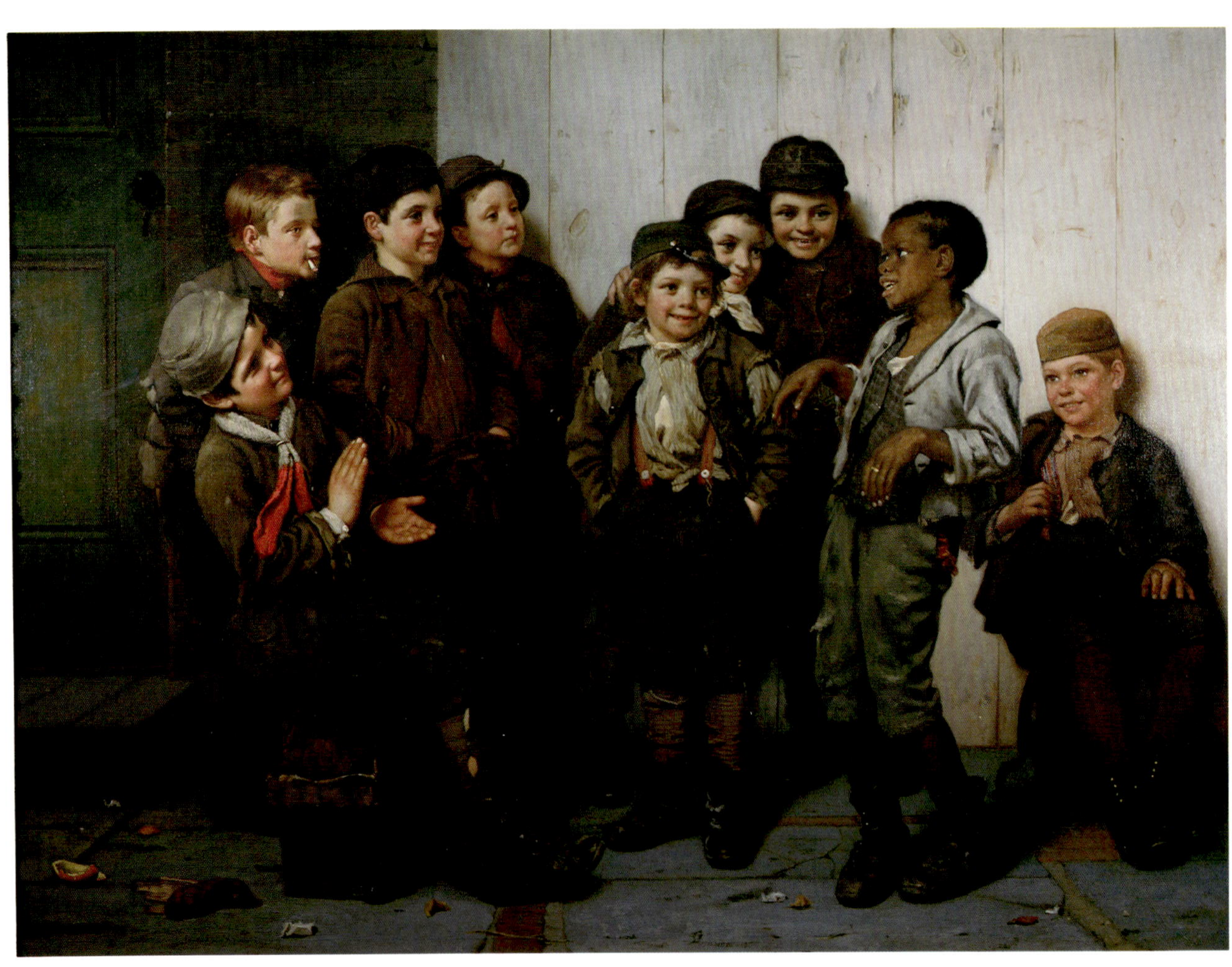

29. **A Jolly Lot,** 1885, Private Collection

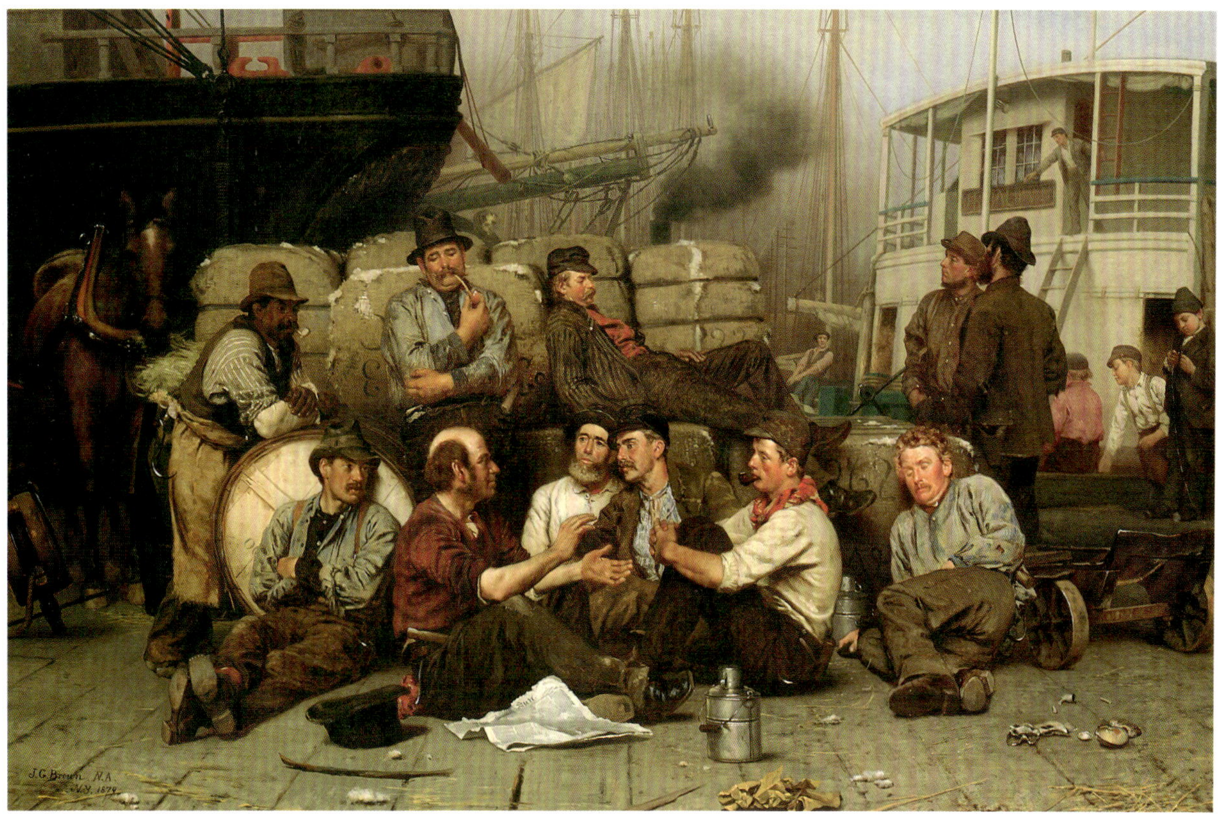

30. **The Longshoremen's Noon,** 1879, In the Collection of The Corcoran Gallery of Art, Museum Purchase, Gallery Fund, 1900

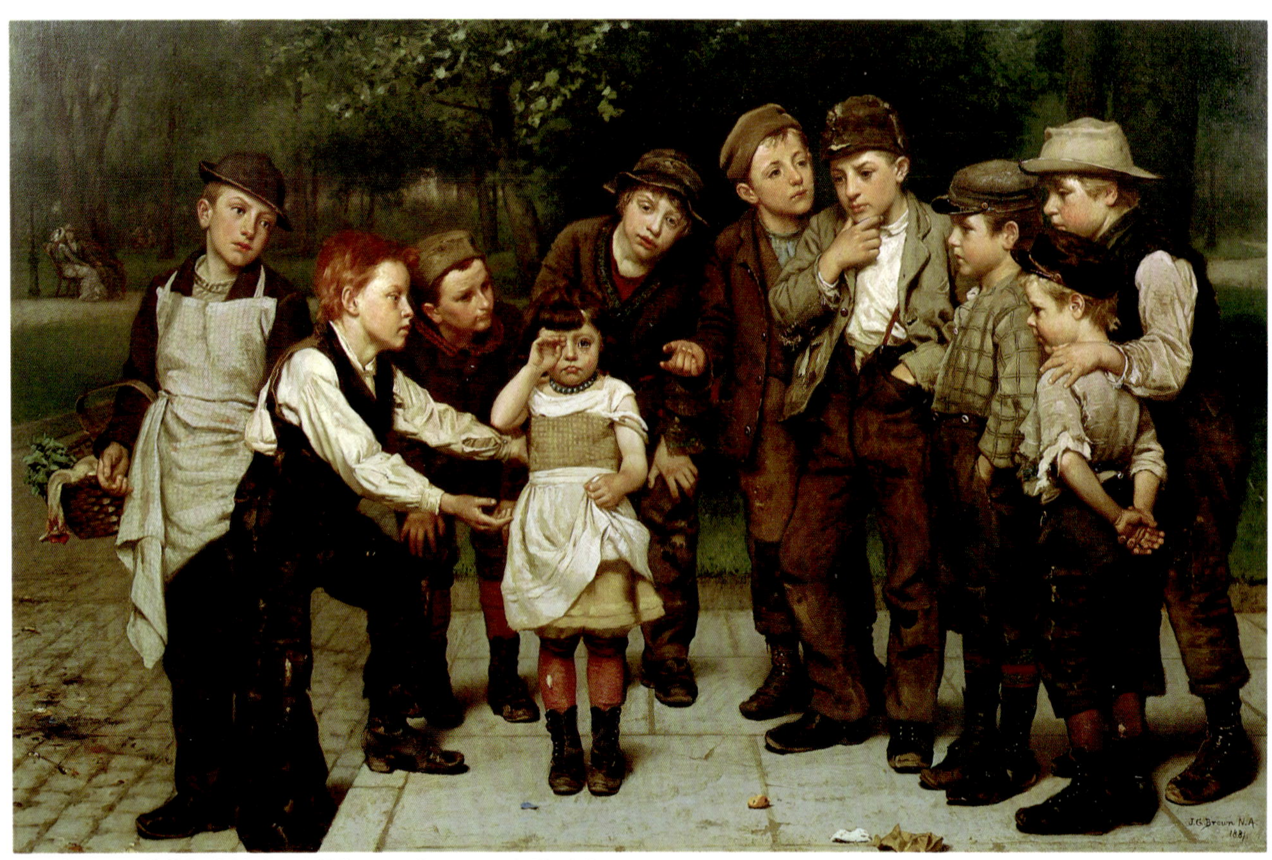

31. **The Lost Child,** 1881, James F. Scott — Greenwood, Virginia

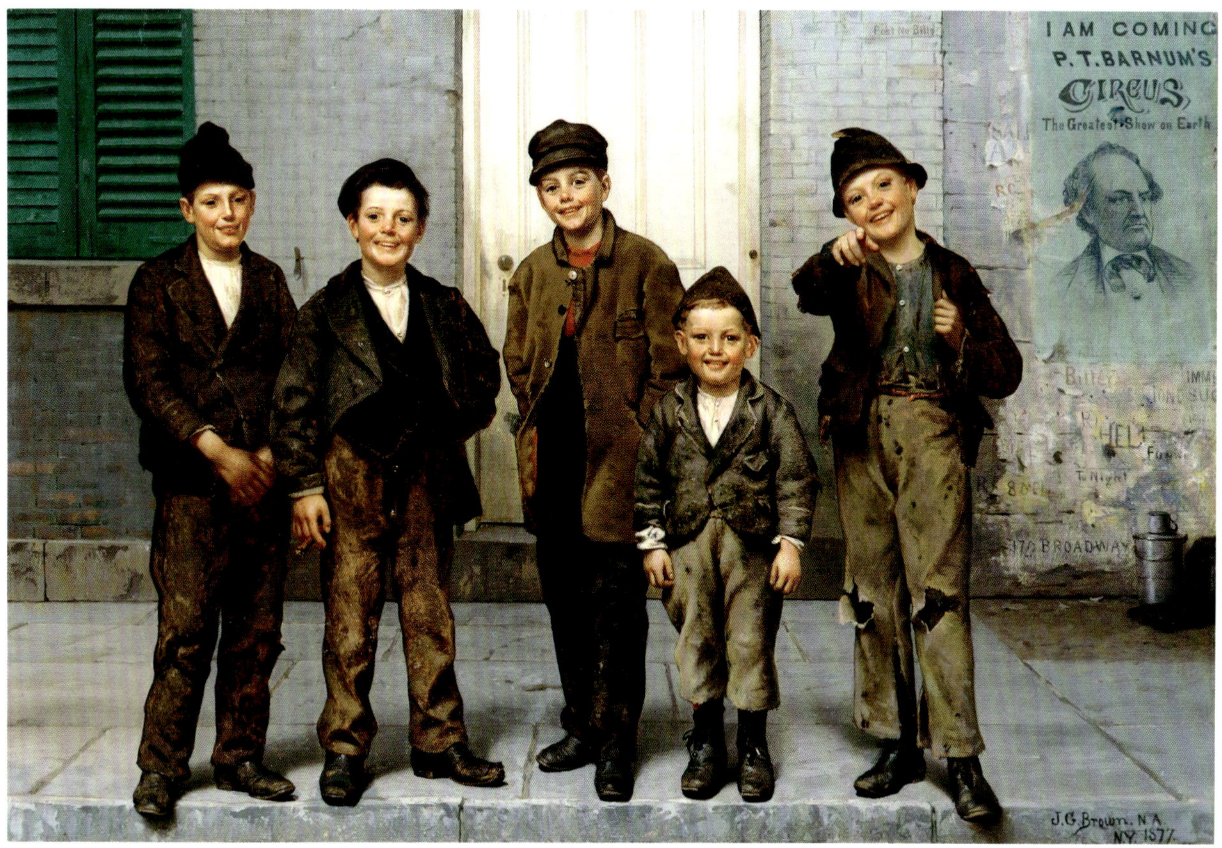

32. **The Passing Show,** 1877, Private Collection

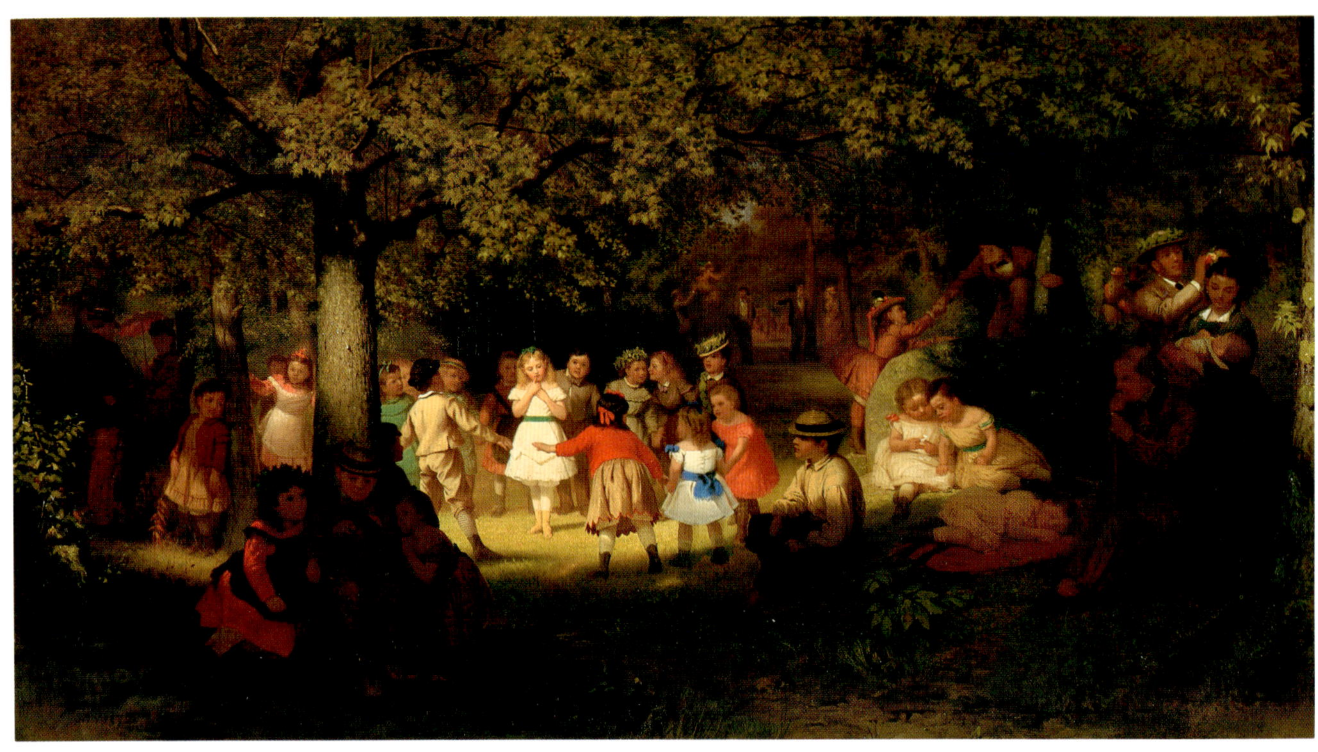

33. **Picnic Party in the Woods,** 1872, Collection of Jo Ann and Julian Ganz, Jr.

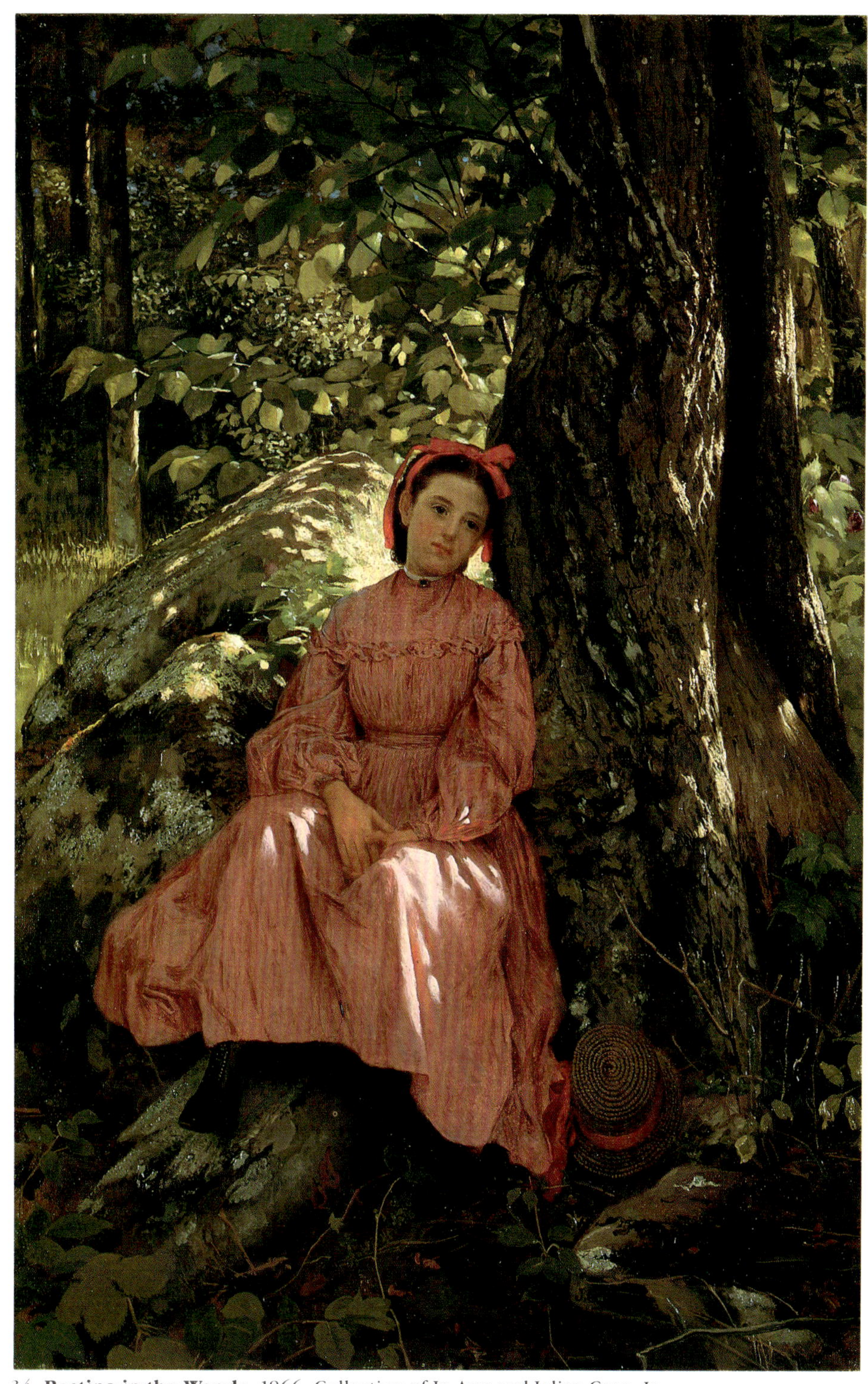

34. **Resting in the Woods,** 1866, Collection of Jo Ann and Julian Ganz, Jr.

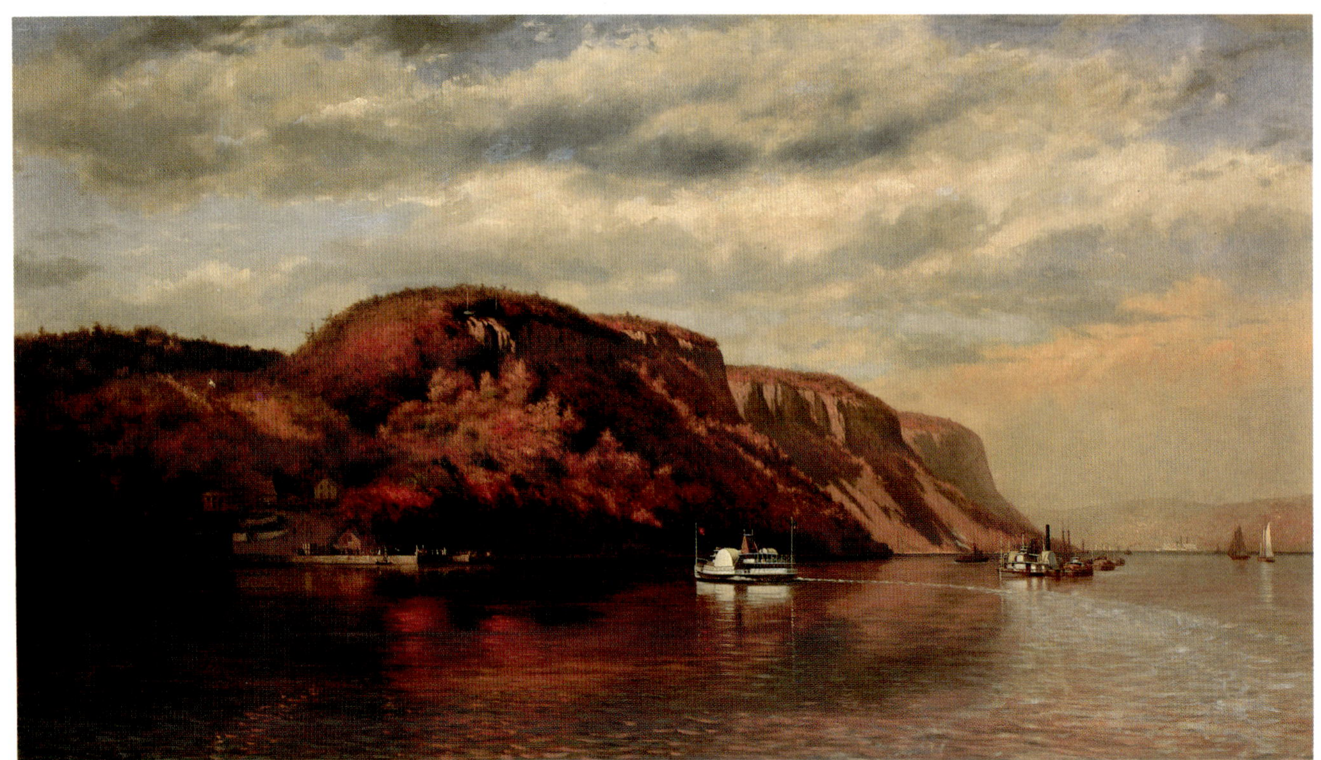

35. **View of the Palisades, Hudson River,** 1867, The Fine Arts Museums of San Francisco, Gift of Mr. & Mrs. John D. Rockefeller 3rd.

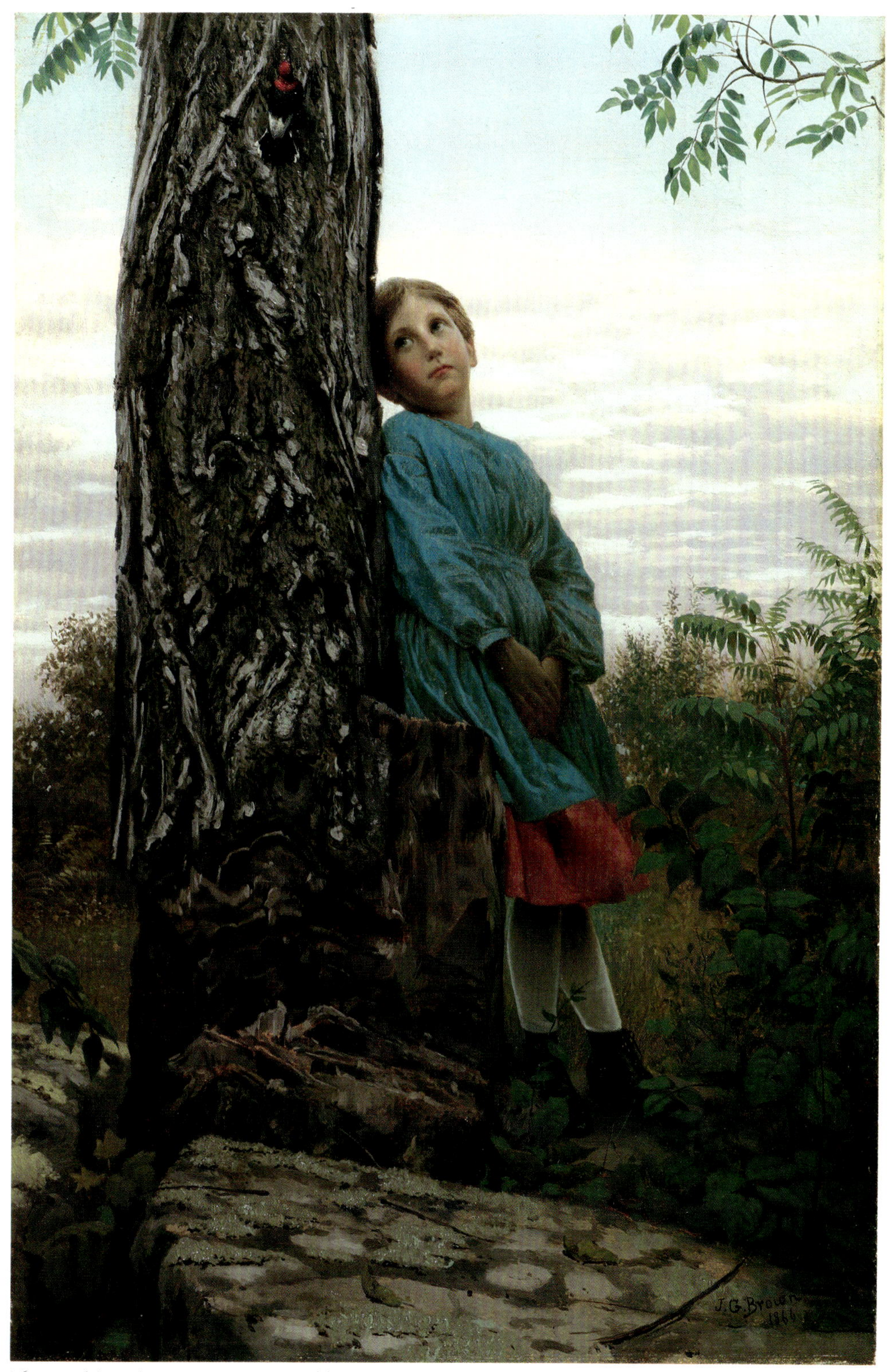

36. **Watching the Woodpecker,** 1866, Private Collection

CHECKLIST

Works are listed alphabetically; all paintings are oil on canvas unless otherwise indicated. Dimensions are given in inches and centimeters, with height preceding width. Original titles, when known, are marked by an asterisk.

1. ***Allegro** and ***Penseroso** 1864, 1865 (framed together; fig. 13)
   Allegro 1864
   Oil on academy board, 6⅝ x 5¾ (16.83 x 14.6)
   Signed l.l.: J.G. Brown / 1864
   In the Collection of The Corcoran Gallery of Art, Gift of William Wilson Corcoran, 1869
   Penseroso 1865
   Oil on wood panel, 6½ x 5⅝ (16.51 x 14.29)
   Signed l.r.: J.G. Brown / 1865
   In the Collection of The Corcoran Gallery of Art, Gift of William Wilson Corcoran, 1869

2. **The Beggars** 1863 (fig. 12)
   15⅛ x 12⅛ (38.42 x 30.8)
   Signed l.l.: J.G. Brown / N.Y. 1863
   Wichita Art Museum, Wichita, Kansas

3. **The Berry Boy** c. 1877 (fig. 11)
   23 x 15 (58.42 x 38)
   Signed l.l.: J.G. Brown. N.A.
   George Walter Vincent Smith Art Museum, Springfield, Massachusetts

4. **The Boot-black** 1878 (fig. 16)
   15 x 11 (38.1 x 27.94)
   Signed l.l.: J.G. Brown. N.A. / 1878.
   Wadsworth Atheneum, Hartford, CT. Bequest of Ambrose Spencer

5. **Buy a Posy** c. 1881 (fig. 18)
   23⅛ x 15¼ (58.73 x 38.73)
   Signed l.l.: J.G. Brown. N.A.
   North Carolina Museum of Art, Raleigh, Given in memory of Mr. and Mrs. E.J. Ellisberg by their children

6. **By the Forest Brook** 1875 (fig. 37)
   29 15/16 x 25 (76.07 x 63.5)
   Signed l.l.: J.G. Brown. n.a. / 1875.
   Lent by the West Foundation

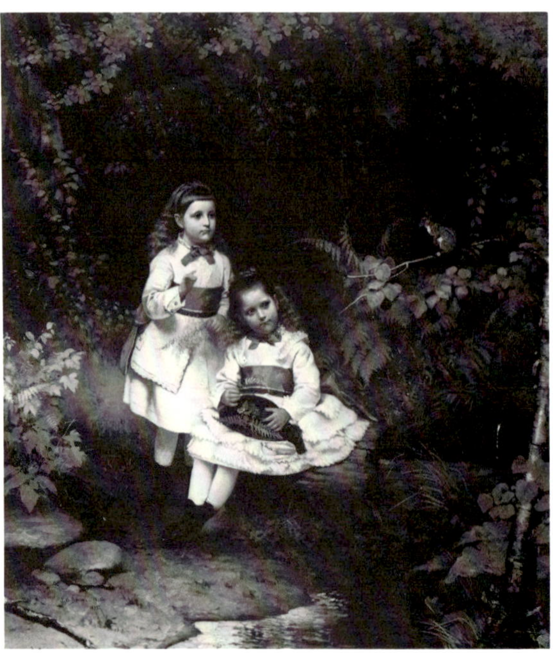

37. Cat. no. 6

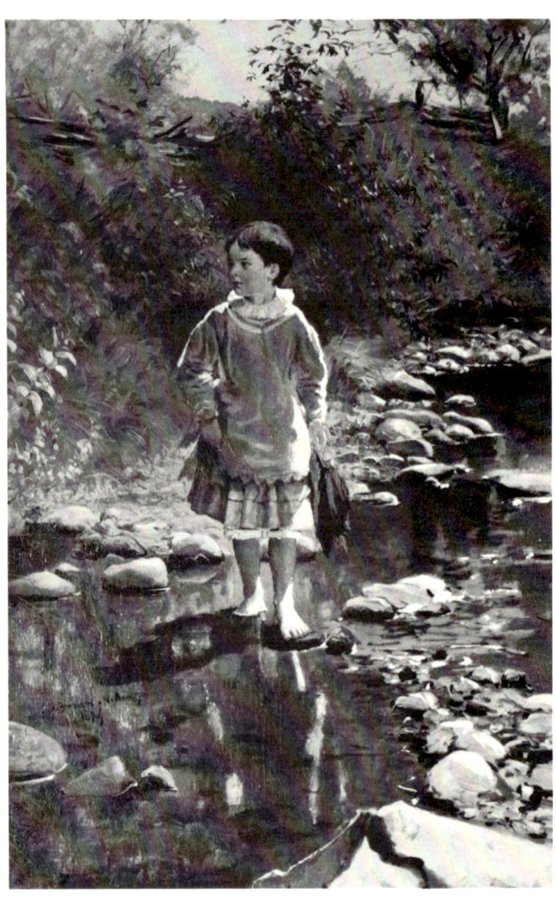

38. Cat. no. 11

7. *__Camp in the Maine Wood, No. 3__ 1879 (fig. 56)
14½ x 23 (36.83 x 58.42)
Signed l.l.: J.G. Brown / 1879
The FORBES Magazine Collection, New York

8. **The Cider Mill** 1880 (fig. 25)
30 x 24 (76.2 x 60.96)
Signed l.r.: J.G. Brown. N.A. / 1880.
Daniel J. Terra Collection. Terra Museum of American Art, Chicago

9. *__Claiming the Shot: After the Hunt in the Adirondacks__ 1865 (fig. 5)
32 x 50 (81.28 x 127)
Signed l.l.: J.G. Brown / N.Y. 1865
The Detroit Institute of Arts, Founders Society Purchase, Robert H. Tannahill Foundation Fund

10. *__The Country Gallants__ 1876 (fig. 26)
30¹⁄₁₆ x 46 (76.36 x 116.84)
Signed l.r.: J.G. Brown N.A. / N.Y. 1876
The Toledo Museum of Art; Gift of Florence Scott Libbey

11. *__Crossing the Brook__ 1874 (fig. 38)
23 x 15 (58.42 x 38.1)
Signed l.l.: J.G. Brown. N.A. / 1874
George Walter Vincent Smith Art Museum, Springfield, Massachusetts

12. *__Extra__ c. 1889 (title page)
25 x 30 (63.5 x 76.2)
Signed l.l.: copyright / J.G. Brown N.A.
Dr. and Mrs. Kenneth Blau

13. *__Fishing, Fort Lee, New Jersey__ c. 1870 's (fig. 39)
17 x 22½ (43.18 x 57.15)
Signed l.r.: J.G. Brown N.A.
Mrs. Charles Shoemaker

14. *__Fresh-Water Sailor__ 1875 (fig. 40)
Watercolor on paper, 17½ x 12⅛ (44.45 x 30.80)
Signed l.r.: J.G. Brown. / 1875.
Mr. and Mrs. Norman Schnee

15. *__Gathering Autumn Leaves__ 1875 (fig. 10)
30⅛ x 25 (76.52 x 63.5)
Signed l.r.: J.G. Brown. / 1875.
Private Collection

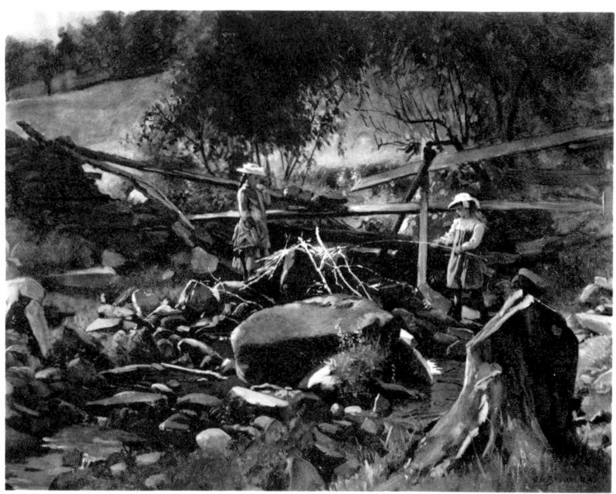

39. Cat. no. 13

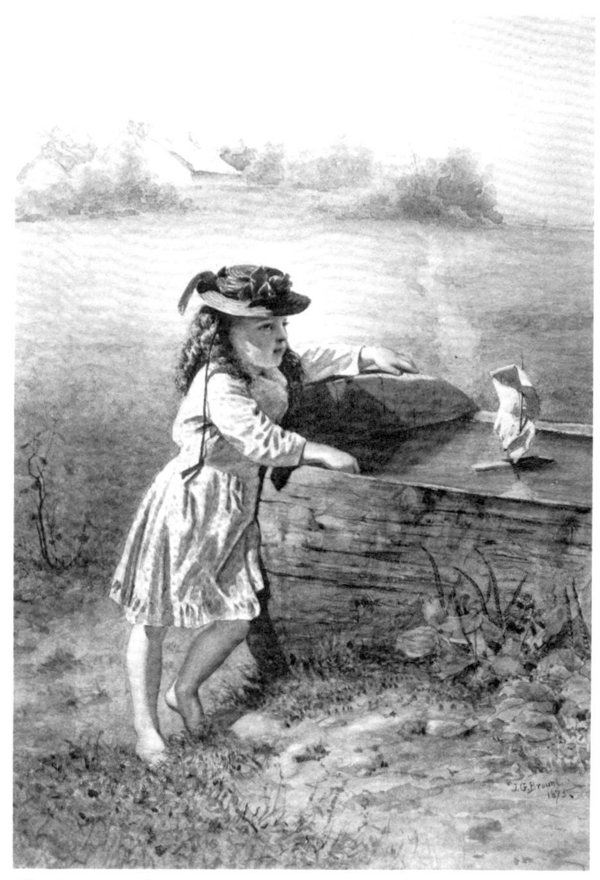

40. Cat. no. 14

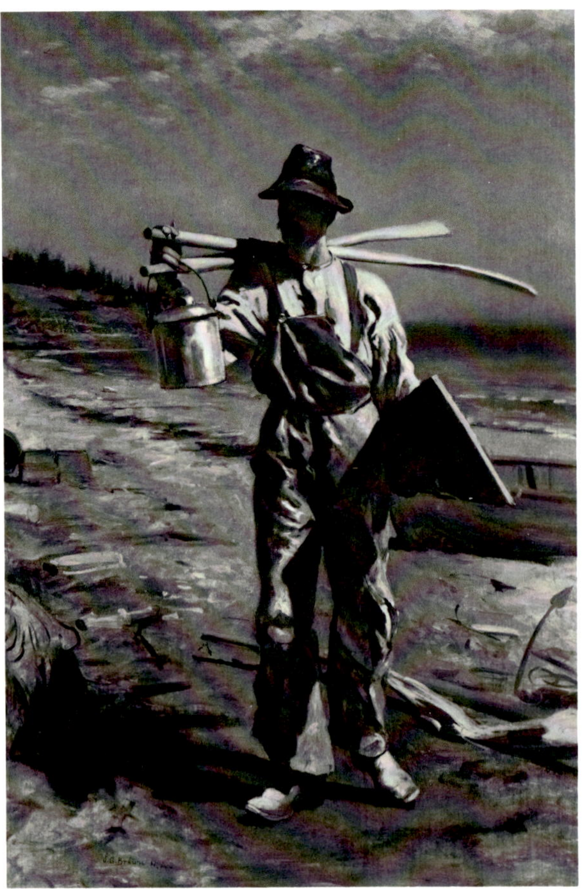

41. Cat. no. 16

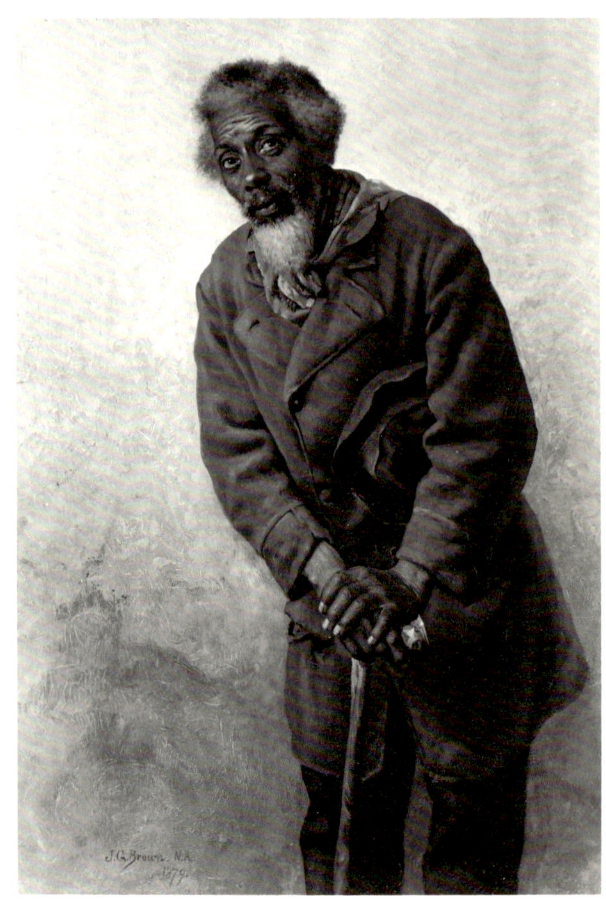

42. Cat. no. 17

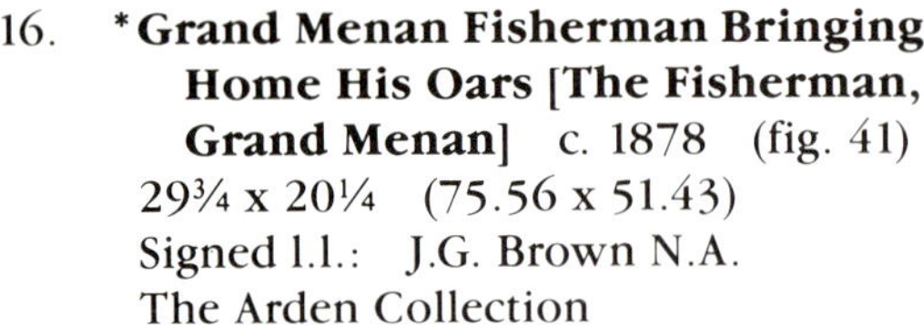

16. ***Grand Menan Fisherman Bringing Home His Oars [The Fisherman, Grand Menan]** c. 1878 (fig. 41)
29¾ x 20¼ (75.56 x 51.43)
Signed l.l.: J.G. Brown N.A.
The Arden Collection

17. ***Hard Times, Massa** 1879 (fig. 42)
30 x 20 (76.2 x 50.8)
Signed l.l.: J.G. Brown. N.A. / 1879.
Collection of Mr. and Mrs. Thomas Davies

18. **The Harpist [*"A Sweet Singer in Israel"]** 1870 (fig. 27)
30 x 25¼ (76.2 x 64.13)
Signed l.l.: J.G. Brown / 1870
Private Collection

19. ***Hiding in the Old Oak** 1874 (fig. 9)
30 x 25⅛ (76.2 x 63.82)
Signed l.r.: J.G. Brown. / 1874.
St. Johnsbury Athenaeum

20. ***Home Comforts** c. 1893 (fig. 23)
35 x 40 (88.9 x 101.6)
Signed l.l.: J.G. Brown N.A.
Charles and Ann Spaulding

21. ***The Industrious Family** c. 1890's (fig. 28)
25 x 30 (63.5 x 76.2)
Signed l.l.: J.G. Brown N.A.
Marge and Leslie Greenbaum

22. ***Jersey Mud** c. 1885-1890 (fig. 20)
23¼ x 15¾ (61.3 x 41)
Signed l.r.: Copyright / J.G. Brown N.A.
Lent by the High Museum of Art, Atlanta, Georgia; gift of Mr. and Mrs. George E. Missbach

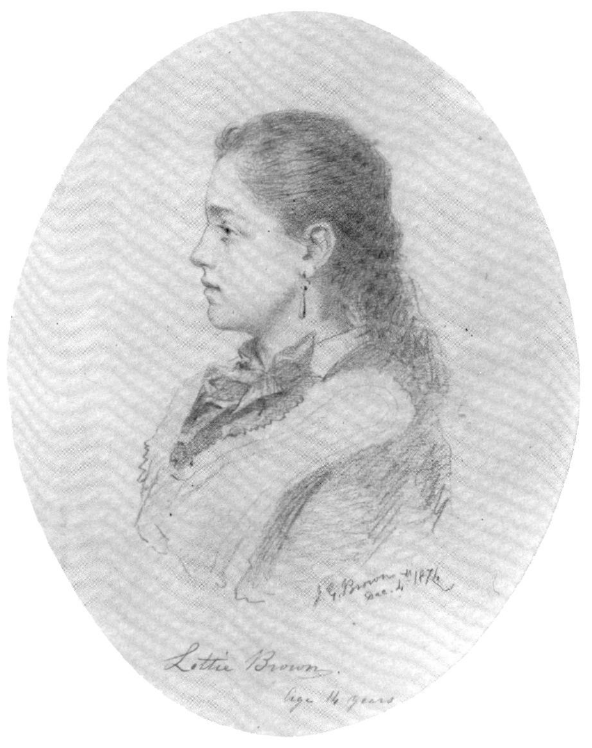

43. Cat. no. 27

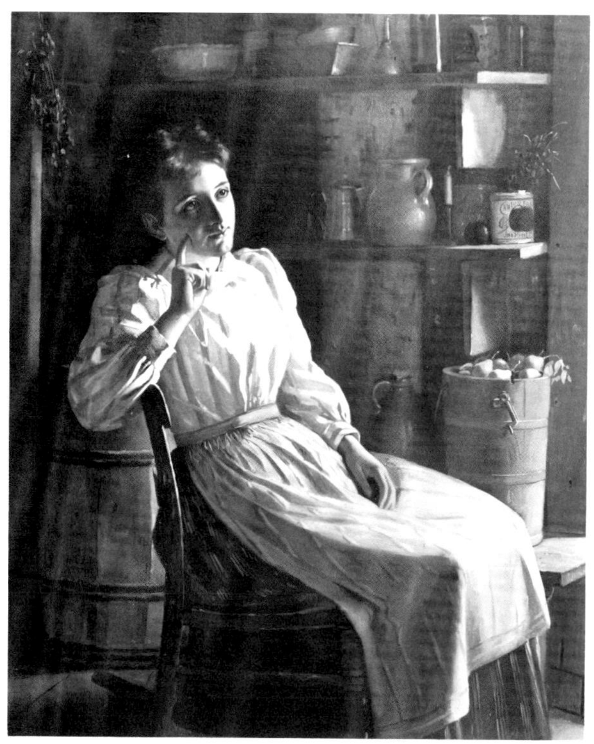

44. Cat. no. 28

23. ***A Jolly Lot** 1885 (fig. 29)
32¼ x 44¼ (81.91 x 112.39)
Signed l.l.: J.G. Brown N.A./1885.
Private Collection

24. ***The Little Queen of the Woods** 1865 (fig. 6)
20 x 15 (50.8 x 38.1)
Signed l.l.: J.G. Brown./1865
The Jones Library, Inc., Amherst, Mass.

25. ***The Longshoremen's Noon** 1879 (fig. 30)
33¼ x 50¼ (84.45 x 127.63)
Signed l.l.: J.G. Brown. N.A./N.Y. 1879.
In the Collection of The Corcoran Gallery of Art, Museum Purchase, Gallery Fund, 1900

26. ***The Lost Child** 1881 (fig. 31)
29 x 44 (73.7 x 111.76)
Signed l.r.: J.G. Brown N.A./1881.
James F. Scott—Greenwood, Virginia

27. ***Lottie Brown** 1874 (fig. 43)
Pencil on paper, 9½ x 7½ (24.13 x 19.05)
Signed l.r.: J.G. Brown/Dec. 4th 1874
Inscribed l.c.: Lottie Brown./Age 14 years.
The Arden Collection

28. ***Meditation** c. 1890's (fig. 44)
30 x 25 (76.2 x 63.5)
Signed l.l.: J.G. Brown/N.A.
Lent by The Metropolitan Museum of Art; G.A. Hearn Fund, 1909.

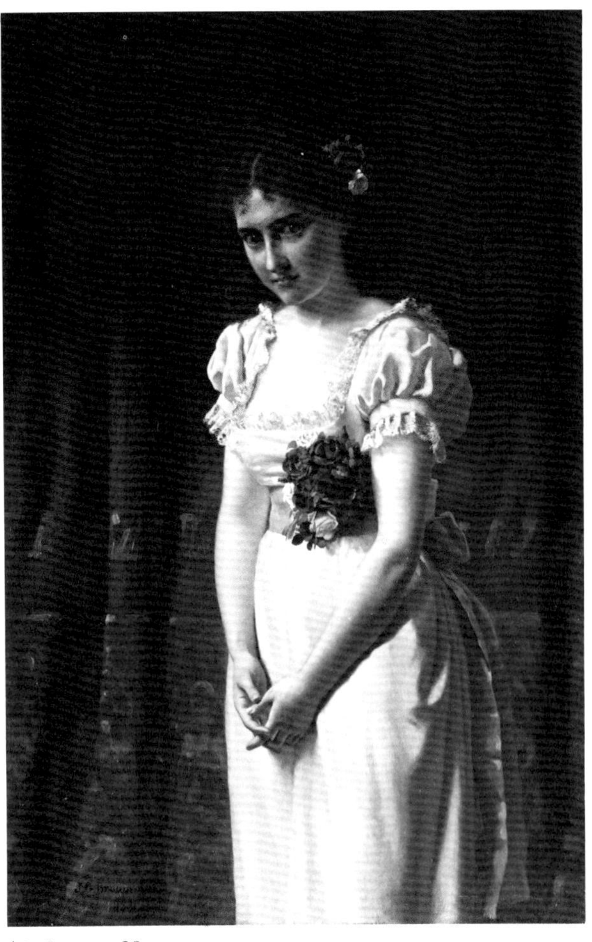

45. Cat. no. 29

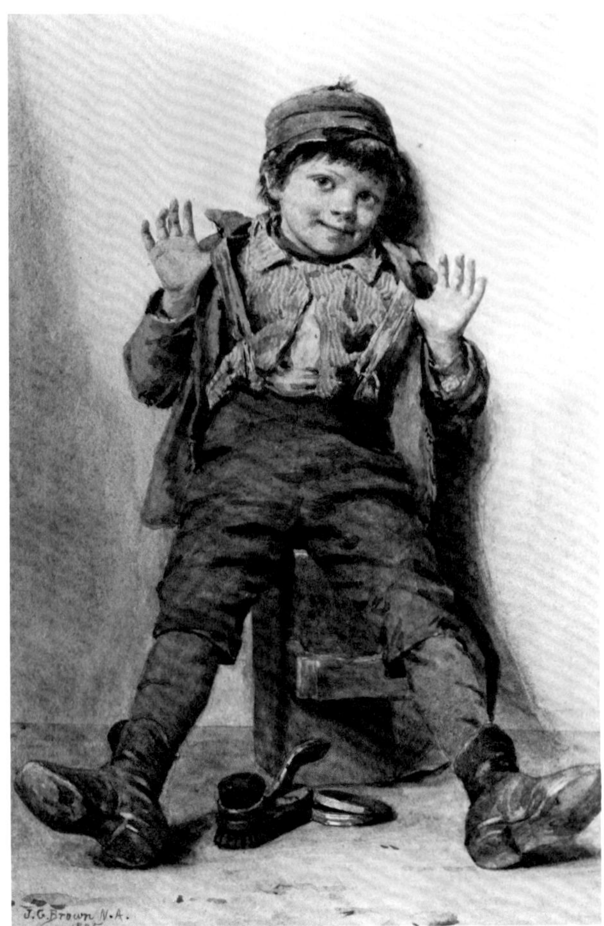

46. Cat. no. 35

29. **Meditation** 1881 (fig. 45)
30 x 20 (76.2 x 50.8)
Signed l.l.: J.G. Brown N.A. / 1881.
Indianapolis Museum of Art: Dr. Frank C. Wicks Memorial Fund

30. **The Music Lesson** 1870 (fig. 8)
24 x 20 (61 x 50.8)
Signed l.l.: J.G. Brown/N.Y. 1870
Lent by The Metropolitan Museum of Art; Gift of Colonel Charles A. Fowler, 1921

31. ***The Neighbors** 1881 (fig. 22)
25 x 30 (63.5 x 76.2)
Signed l.r.: J.G. Brown N.A. / 1881.
Lent by the High Museum of Art, Atlanta, Georgia; gift of Mr. and Mrs. George E. Missbach

32. **Paddy's Valentine** 1885 (fig. 17)
24 x 16 (60.96 x 40.64)
Signed l.r.: J.G. Brown. N.A. / 1885
Mr. and Mrs. Norman Schnee

33. ***The Passing Show** 1877 (fig. 32)
20 x 30 (50.8 x 76.2)
Signed l.r.: J.G. Brown. N.A. / N.Y. 1877.
Private Collection

34. ***Pay Toll** 1862 (fig. 2)
15 x 12 (38.1 x 30.48)
Signed l.l.: J.G. Brown 1862
Private Collection

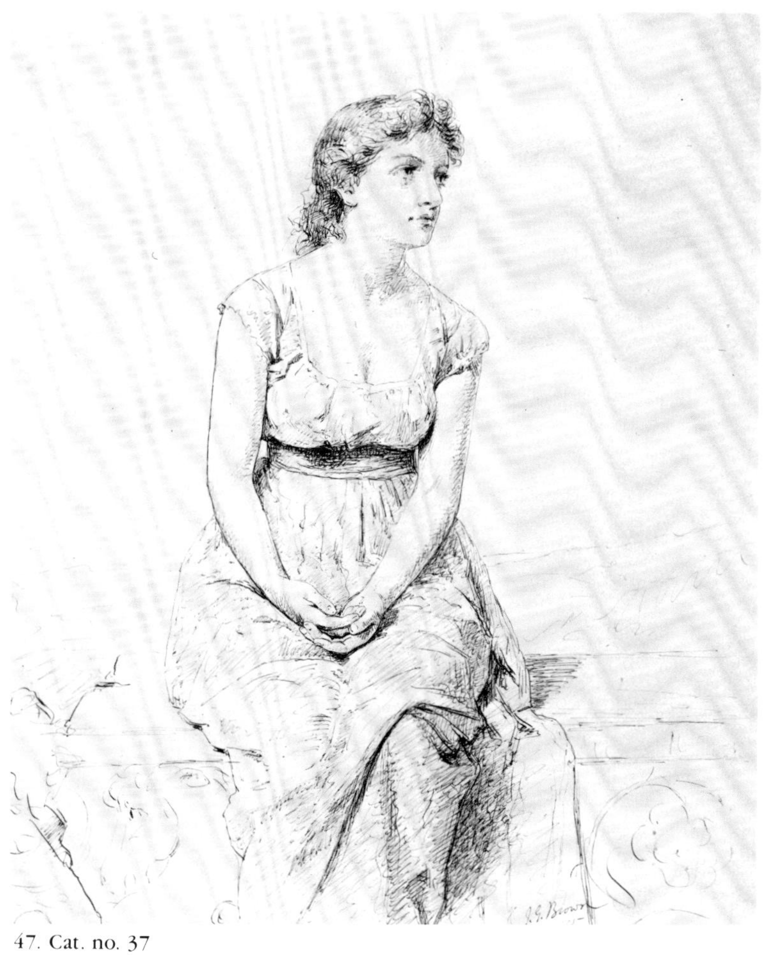

47. Cat. no. 37

35. *Perfectly Happy 1885 (fig. 46)
Watercolor on paper, 20 x 13 (50.8 x 33.02)
Signed l.l.: J.G. Brown N.A. / 1885
The Butler Institute of American Art, Youngstown, Ohio

36. *Picnic Party in the Woods 1872 (fig. 33)
24 x 44 (60.96 x 111.76)
Signed l.l.: J.G. Brown. / N.Y. 1872.
Collection of Jo Ann and Julian Ganz, Jr.

37. **Portrait of a Young Woman** 1885 (fig. 47)
Pen and ink on paper, 16 x 12⅝ (40.64 x 32.07)
Signed l.r.: J.G. Brown / 1885
Childs Gallery, Ltd., Boston & New York

38. **Pulling for Shore [*Pull for the Shore]** 1878 (fig. 21)
34¼ x 56⅛ (86.99 x 142.56)
Signed l.r.: J.G. Brown N.A. / 1878.
The Chrysler Museum, Norfolk, Virginia, Gift of Walter P. Chrysler, Jr.

39. ***Resting in the Woods** 1866 (fig. 34)
18⅜ x 12⅛ (46.67 x 30.8)
Signed l.r.: J.G. Brown / 1866
Collection of Jo Ann and Julian Ganz, Jr.

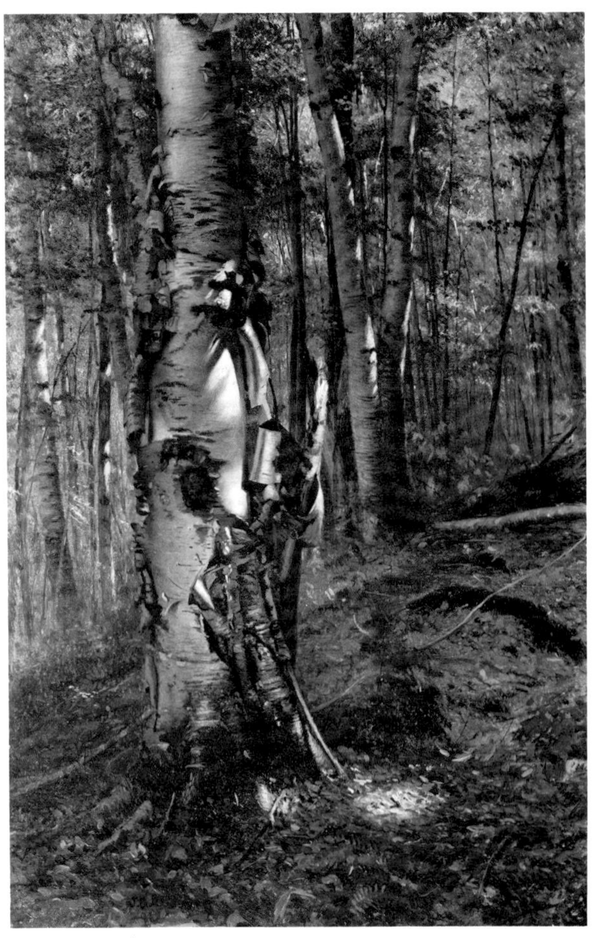

48. Cat. no. 41

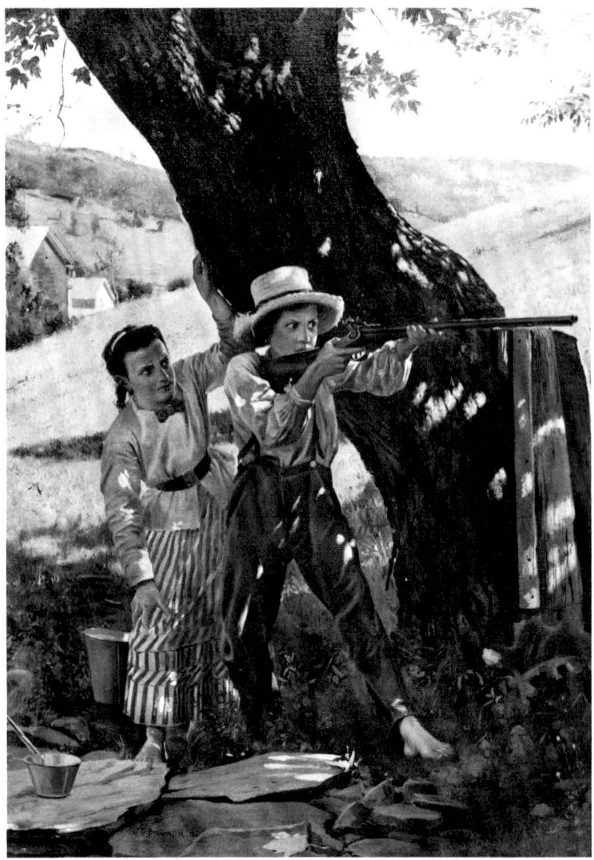

49. Cat. no. 42

40. *The Sidewalk Dance 1894 (fig. 24)
40¼ x 60 (102.23 x 152.4)
Signed l.l.: copyright/J.G. Brown N.A./1894
Private Collection

41. **Silver Birches** 1864 (fig. 48)
21½ x 13½ (54.61 x 34.29)
Signed l.l.: J.G. Brown/1864
Hirschl and Adler Galleries, Inc., New York

42. ***A Sure Shot** c. 1872-1875 (fig. 49)
21 x 15 (53.34 x 38.1)
Signed l.l.: J.G. Brown. n.a.
The Brooklyn Museum, Dick S. Ramsay Fund 48.139

43. **The Teacher** 1866 (fig. 14)
16 x 26 (40.64 x 66.04)
Signed l.r.: J.G. Brown./N.Y. 1866
Anonymous Loan

44. **A Tough Story** 1886 (fig. 19)
25 x 30 (63.5 x 76.2)
Signed l.l.: J.G. Brown N.A./1886.
North Carolina Museum of Art, Raleigh

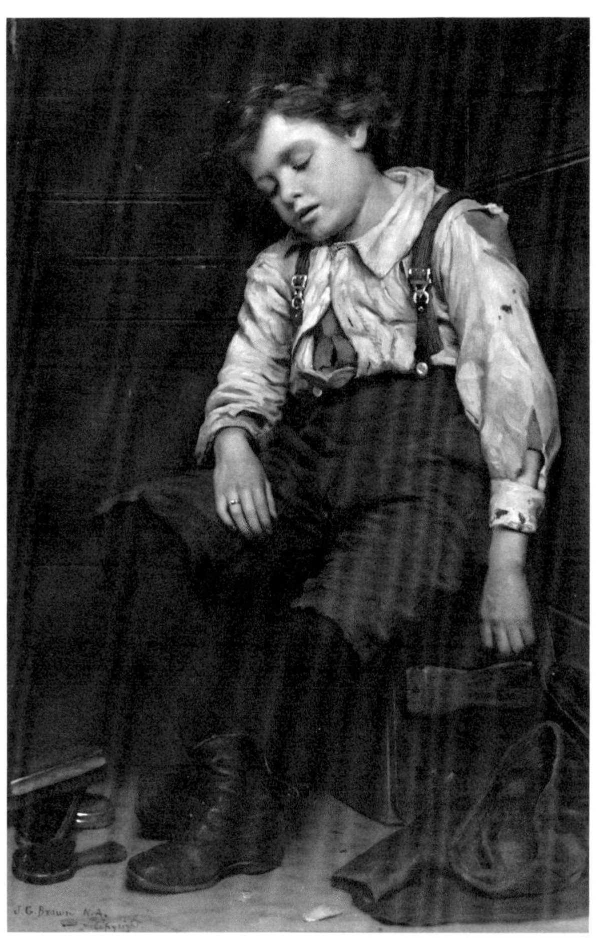

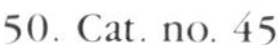
50. Cat. no. 45

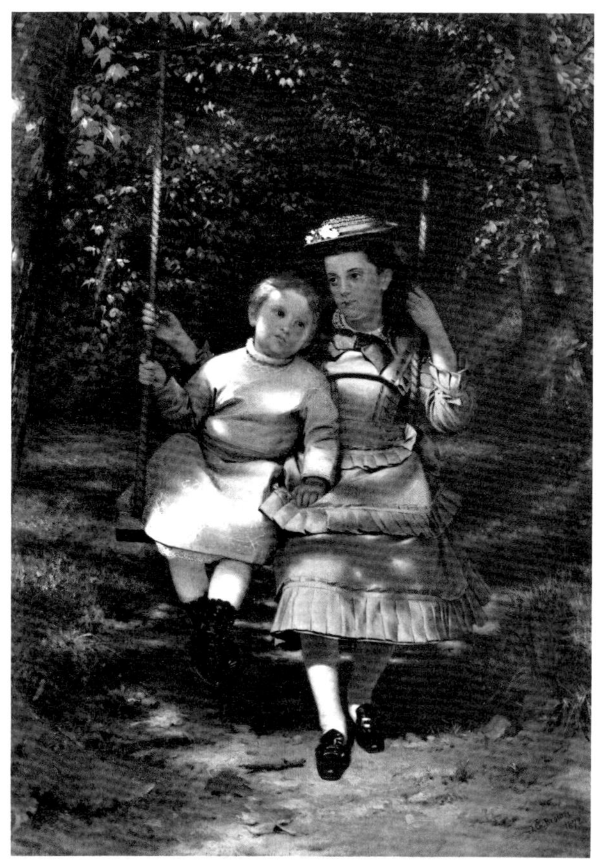

51. Cat. no. 46

45. **Tuckered Out—The Shoeshine Boy**
c. 1888 (fig. 50)
24 x 16 (61 x 40.6)
Signed l.l.: J.G. Brown N.A./Copyright.
Museum of Fine Arts, Boston. Bequest of Maxim Karolik 64.467

46. **Two Girls on a Swing** 1872 (fig. 51)
17⅞ x 13⅞ (45.4 x 35.24)
Signed l.r.: J.G. Brown./1872.
Mr. and Mrs. Andrew J. Goodman

47. ***The Victim** 1861 (fig. 3)
14 x 12 (35.56 x 30.48)
Signed l.l.: J.G. Brown/1861
National Academy of Design, New York

48. **View of the Palisades, Hudson River**
1867 (fig. 35)
39 x 72 (99.06 x 182.88)
Signed l.l.: J.G. Brown./N.Y. 1867
The Fine Arts Museums of San Francisco, Gift of Mr. & Mrs. John D. Rockefeller 3rd.

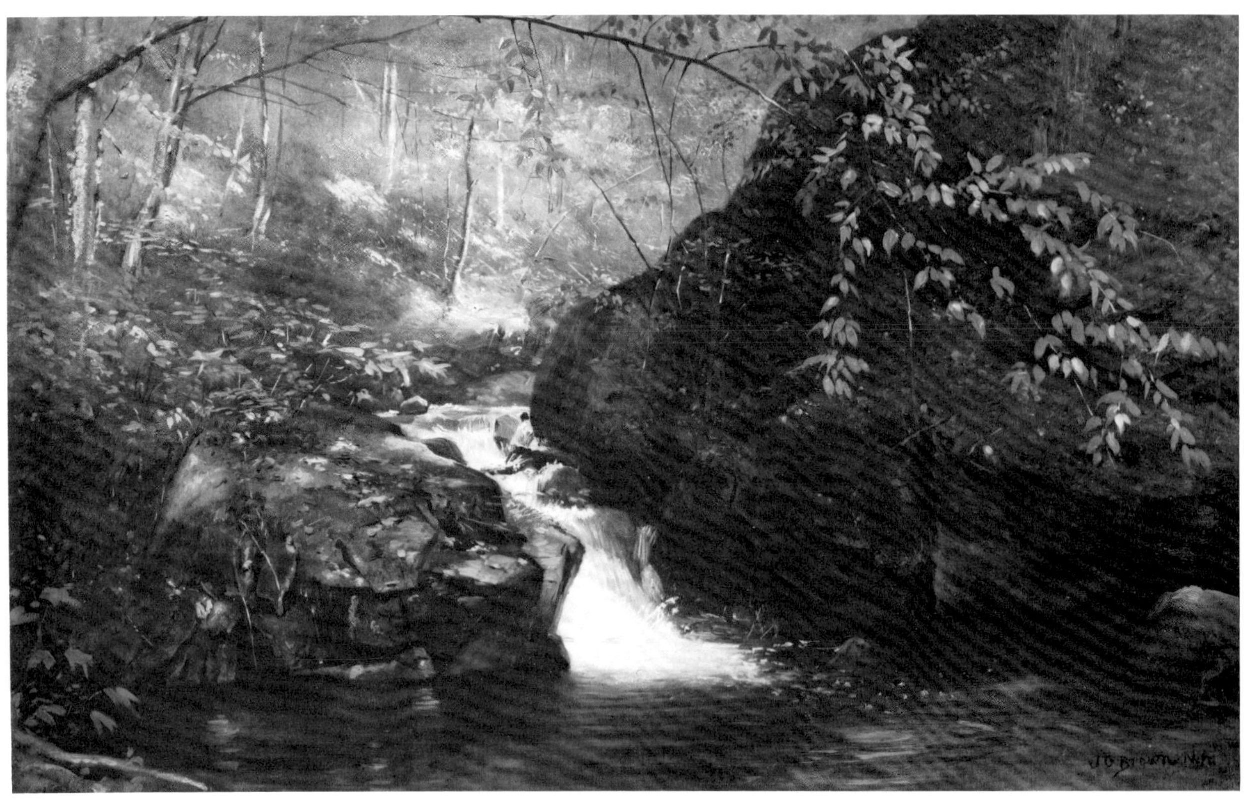

52. Cat. no. 51

49. ***Walk In** c. 1875 (fig. 57)
23⅝ x 15 (60.1 x 38.1)
Signed l.r.: J.G. Brown
Hirschl and Adler Galleries, Inc., New York

50. ***Watching the Woodpecker** 1866 (fig. 36)
18 x 12 (45.72 x 30.48)
Signed l.r.: J.G. Brown/1866
Private Collection

51. ***Waterfall, Huntington, Massachusetts** c. 1874 (fig. 52)
14¾ x 23⅝ (37.46 x 60.1)
Signed l.r.: J.G. Brown N.A.
D. Wigmore Fine Art, Inc., New York

52. ***Weighing Fish** 1878 (fig. 53)
30 x 20½ (76.2 x 52.07)
Signed l.r.: J.G. Brown/1878.
The Daniel B. Grossman Galleries, New York, New York

53. ***What's Your Name?** 1876 (fig. 54)
30 x 20 (76.2 x 50.8)
Signed l.r.: J.G. Brown N.A./N.Y. 1876.
The Shearson Lehman Brothers Collection

54. ***When Greek Meets Greek, Then Comes the Tug of War [The Quarrel]** 1866 (fig. 15)
15⅛ x 12 (38.42 x 30.48)
Signed l.l.: J.G. Brown./1866
Mr. and Mrs. Charles B. Tyler

55. **The Young Fisherman** 1877 (fig. 55)
21 x 17 (53.34 x 43.18)
Signed l.l.: J.G. Brown. N.A./1877.
Mrs. Charles Shoemaker

56. **Young Girl in a New York Garden** 1871 (cover)
23¾ x 18⅛ (60.32 x 46.04)
Signed l.r.: J.G. Brown./30th St. N.Y./1871.
From the Private Collection of Mr. and Mrs. Charles O. Smith, Jr.

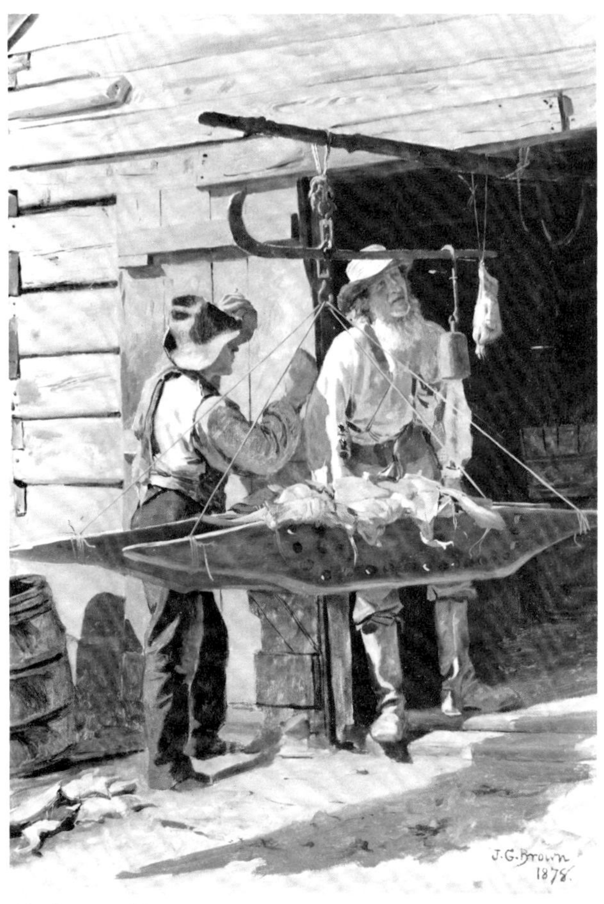

53. Cat. no. 52

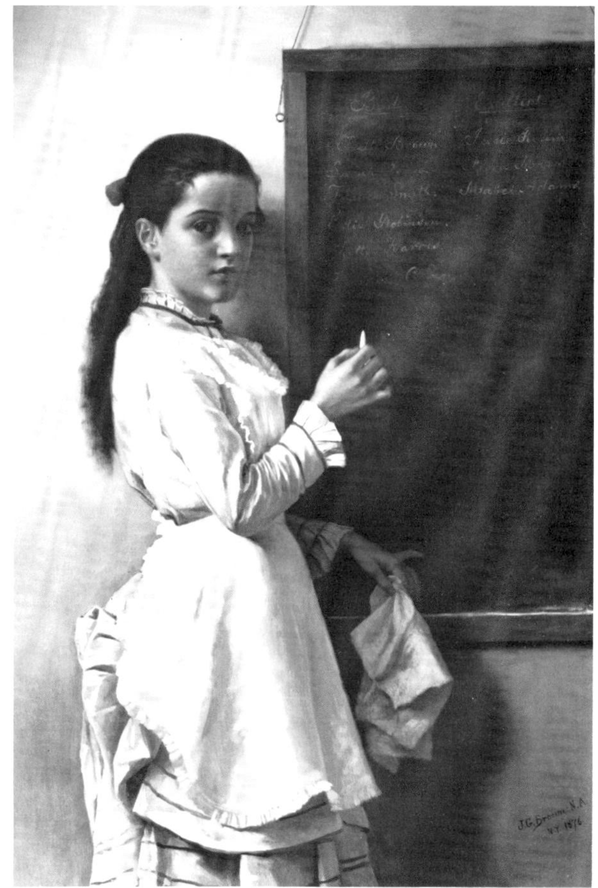

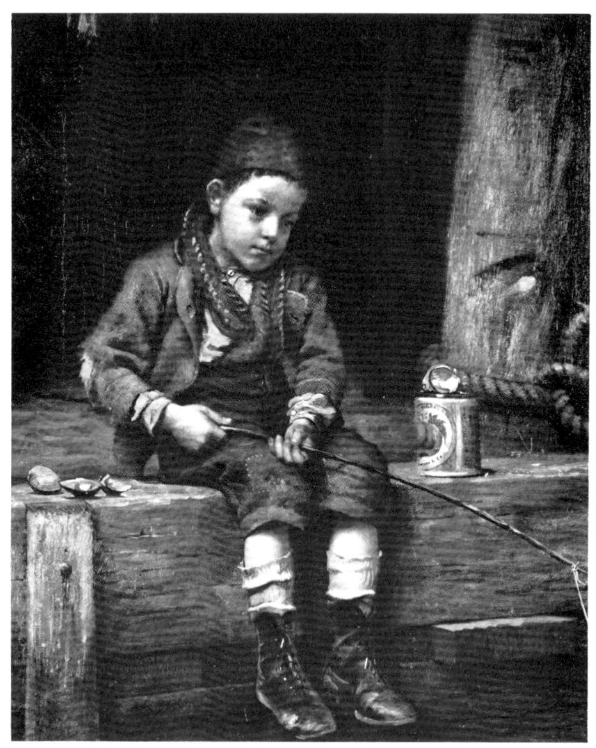

54. (upper right) Cat. no. 53

55. (lower right) Cat. no. 55

LENDERS TO THE EXHIBITION

The Arden Collection

Dr. and Mrs. Kenneth Blau

The Brooklyn Museum, Brooklyn, New York

The Butler Institute of American Art, Youngstown, Ohio

Childs Gallery, Ltd., Boston and New York

The Corcoran Gallery of Art, Washington, D.C.

The Chrysler Museum, Norfolk, Virginia

Collection of Mr. and Mrs. Thomas Davies

The Detroit Institute of Arts, Detroit, Michigan

The Fine Arts Museums of San Francisco, San Francisco, California

The FORBES Magazine Collection, New York

Collection of Jo Ann and Julian Ganz, Jr.

George Walter Vincent Smith Art Museum, Springfield, Massachusetts

Mr. and Mrs. Andrew J. Goodman

Marge and Leslie Greenbaum

The Daniel B. Grossman Galleries, New York

High Museum of Art, Atlanta, Georgia

Hirschl and Adler Galleries, Inc., New York

Indianapolis Museum of Art, Indianapolis, Indiana

The Jones Library, Inc., Amherst, Massachusetts

The Metropolitan Museum of Art, New York

Museum of Fine Arts, Boston, Massachusetts

National Academy of Design, New York

North Carolina Museum of Art, Raleigh, North Carolina

Private Collections

St. Johnsbury Athenaeum, St. Johnsbury, Vermont

Mr. and Mrs. Norman Schnee

James F. Scott, Greenwood, Virginia

The Shearson Lehman Brothers Collection

Mrs. Charles Shoemaker

Collection of Mr. and Mrs. Charles O. Smith, Jr.

Charles and Ann Spaulding

Terra Museum of American Art, Chicago, Illinois

The Toledo Museum of Art, Toledo, Ohio

Mr. and Mrs. Charles B. Tyler

Wadsworth Atheneum, Hartford, Connecticut

West Foundation

Wichita Art Museum, Wichita, Kansas

D. Wigmore Fine Art, Inc., New York

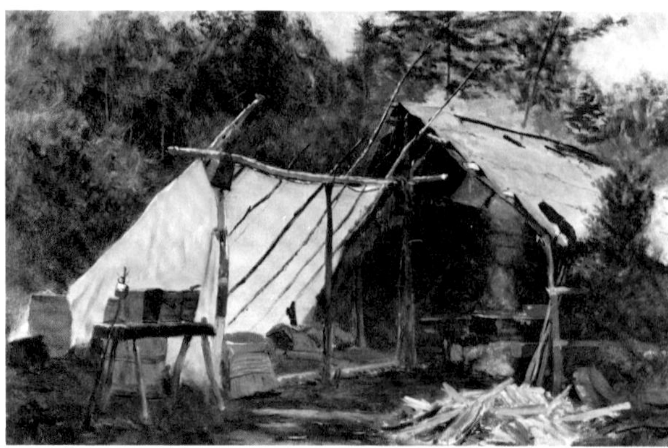

56. **Camp in the Maine Wood, No. 3,** 1879, The FORBES Magazine Collection, New York

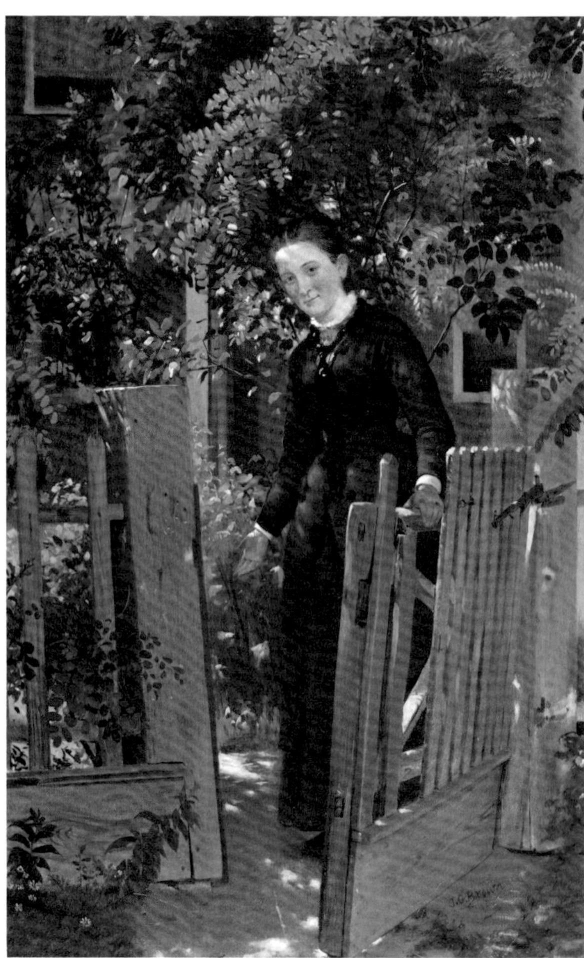

57. **Walk In,** c. 1875, Hirschl and Adler Galleries, Inc., New York